EBONICS IS GOOD

BY
DR. ABDUL KARIM BANGURA
Howard University

cognella™
San Diego, CA

First published in the United States of America in 2011 by Cognella, a division of University Readers, Inc.

Trademark Notice: Product or corporate names may be trademarks or registered trademarks, and are used only for identification and explanation without intent to infringe.

15 14 13 12 11   1 2 3 4 5

Printed in the United States of America

ISBN: 978-1-60927-901-1

www.cognella.com   800.200.3908

DEDICATION

To The Afrikan, Who Must Endure!

CONTENTS

ACKNOWLEDGMENTS

I, and hopefully many readers, owe gratitude to:

Mwalimu/Honorable Teacher Baba Joseph Wallace, for being a true Afrikan Teacher.

Dr. Abdul Aziz Said, for being my revered Mwalimu/Honorable Teacher and tirelessly engaged in smoothing out intellectual rough spots.

Dr. Darrell D. Randall, for being my consummate mentor.

Professors, administrators and staff of American University, Howard University, Bowie State University and Prairie View A&M University, for providing stimulating academic environments to test my ideas.

Students at American University, Howard University, Bowie State University and Prairie View A&M University, for listening to and providing useful comments on the subject. Asking difficult questions often leads to better answers.

Diana Kelly, Fatmata Bangura, Isatu Bangura and the other members of the various families to which I belong, for offering encouragement and prayers.

PREFACE

This book is an expansion of an earlier monograph with the same title published by The African Institution in 1997. It is part and parcel of my humble response to the clarion call of Mwalimu Carter G. Woodson, Mwalimu Frantz Fanon, and Mwalimu Malcolm X, among others, to address our African language question. As the following excerpts from the teachings of these great Africans show, it behooves us to counter the assumption of the ill-informed that Ebonics is "bad" by demonstrating that it is a GOOD language and worthy of respect.

Mwalimu Carter G. Woodson observes in his book, *Miseducation of the Negro*, that (1933:19-22):

> In the study of language in school pupils were made to scoff at the Negro dialect as some peculiar possession of the Negro which they should despise rather than directed to study the background of this language as a broken-down African tongue—in short to understand their own linguistic history, which is certainly more important for them than the study of French Phonetics or Historical Spanish Grammar. To the African language as such no attention was given except in case of the preparation of traders, missionaries and public functionaries to exploit the natives. This number of persons thus trained, of course, constituted a small fraction hardly deserving attention.

> From literature the African was excluded altogether. He was not supposed to have expressed any thought worth knowing. The philosophy in the African proverbs and in the rich folklore of that continent was ignored to give preference to that developed on the distant shores of the Mediterranean. Most missionary teachers of the freedmen, like most men of our time, had never read the interesting books of travel in Africa, and had never heard of the *Tarikh Es-Soudan*.

> In the teaching of fine arts these instructors usually started with Greece by showing how that art was influenced from without, but they omitted the African influence which scientists now regard as significant and dominant in early Hellas. They failed to teach the student the Mediterranean Melting Pot with the Negroes from Africa bringing their wares, their ideas and their blood therein to influence the history of Greece, Carthage, and Rome. Making desire farther to the thought, our teachers either ignored these influences or endeavored to belittle them by working out theories to the contrary.

The bias did not stop at this point, for it invaded the teaching of the professions. Negro law students were told that they belonged to the most criminal element in the country; and an effort was made to justify the procedure in the seats of injustice where law was interpreted as being one thing for the white man and a different thing for the Negro. In constitutional law the spinelessness of the United States Supreme Court in permitting the judicial nullification of the Fourteenth and Fifteenth Amendments was and still is boldly upheld in our law schools.

In medical schools Negroes were likewise convinced of their inferiority in being reminded of their role as germ carriers. The prevalence of syphilis and tuberculosis among Negroes was especially emphasized without showing that these maladies are more deadly among the Negroes for the reason that they are Caucasian diseases; and since these plagues are new to Negroes, these sufferers have not had time to develop against them the immunity which time has permitted in the Caucasian. Other diseases to which Negroes easily fall prey were mentioned to point out the race as an undesirable element when this condition was due to the Negroes' economic and social status. Little emphasis was placed upon the immunity of the Negro from diseases like yellow fever and influenza which are so disastrous to whites. Yet, the whites were not considered inferior because of this differential resistance to these plagues.

In history, of course, the Negro had no place in this curriculum. He was pictured as a human being of the lower order, unable to subject passion to reason, and therefore useful only when made the hewer of wood and the drawer of water for others. No thought was given to the history of Africa except so far as it had been a field of exploitation for the Caucasian. You might study the history as it was offered in our system from the elementary school throughout the university, and you would never hear Africa mentioned except in the negative. You would never thereby learn that Africans first domesticated the sheep, goat, and cow, developed the idea of trial by jury, produced the first stringed instruments, and gave the world its greatest boon in the discovery of iron. You would never know that prior to the Mohammedan invasion about 1000 A.D. these natives in the heart of Africa had developed powerful kingdoms which were later organized as the Songhay Empire on the order of that of the Roman and boasting of similar grandeur.

Thus, Mwalimu Woodson recommends that (1933:149-151):

We should not close any accredited Negro colleges or universities, but we should reconstruct the whole system. We should not eliminate many of the courses now being offered, but we should secure men of vision to give them from the point of view of the people to be served. We should not spend less money for the higher education of the Negro, but should redefine higher education as preparation to think and work out a program to serve the lowly rather than to live as an aristocrat.

Such subjects of certitude as mathematics, of course, would continue and so would most of the work in practical languages and sciences. In theology, literature, social science, and education, however, radical reconstruction is necessary. The old worn-out theories as to man's relation to God and his fellow man, the system of thought which has permitted one man to exploit, oppress, and exterminate another and still be regarded as righteous must be discarded for the new thought of men as brethren and the idea of God as the lover of all mankind.

After Negro students have mastered the fundamentals of English, the principles of composition, and the leading facts in the development of its literature, they should not spend all of their time in advanced work on Shakespeare, Chaucer and Anglo-Saxons. They should direct their attention also to the folklore of the African, to the philosophy in his proverbs, to the development of the Negro in the use of modern language, and to the works of Negro writers.

The leading facts of the history of the world should be studied by all, but of what advantage is it to the Negro student of history to devote all of his time to courses bearing on such despots as Alexander the Great, Caesar, and Napoleon, or to the record of those nations whose outstanding achievement has been rapine, plunder, and murder for world power? Why not study the African background from the point of view of anthropology and history, and then take up sociology as it concerns the Negro peasant or proletarian who is suffering from sufficient ills to supply laboratory work for the most advanced students of the social order? Why not take up economics as reflected by the Negroes of today and work out some remedy for their lack of capital, the absence of cooperative enterprise, and the short life of their establishments. Institutions like Harvard, Yale and Columbia are not going to do these things, and educators influenced by them to the extent that they become blind to the Negro will never serve the race efficiently.

To educate the Negro we must find out exactly what his background is, what he is today, what his possibilities are, and how to begin with him as he is and make him a better individual of the kind that he is. Instead of cramming the Negro's mind with what others have shown that they can do, we should develop his latent powers that he may perform in society a part of which others are not capable.

As Mwalimu Frantz Fanon explains in the opening paragraph of his book, *Black Skin White Masks* (1967:17-18),

I ascribe a basic importance to the phenomenon of language. That is why I find it necessary to begin with this subject, which should provide us with one of the elements in the colored man's comprehension of the dimension of *the other*. For it is implicit that to speak is to exist absolutely for the other...To speak means to be in a position to use a certain syntax, to grasp the morphology of this or that language, but it means above all to assume a culture, to support the weight of a civilization.

And Mwalimu Malcolm X recounts in his *Malcolm X On Afro-American History* (1967:44-46) that:

The slave maker knew that he couldn't make these people slaves until he first made them dumb. And one of the best ways to make a man dumb is to take his tongue, take his language. A man who can't talk, what do they call him? A dummy. Once your language is gone, you are a dummy. You can't communicate with people who are your relatives, you can never have access to information from your family—you just can't communicate.

Also, if you'll notice, the natural tongue that one speaks is referred to as one's mother tongue—mother tongue. And the natural intelligence that a person has before he goes to school is called mother wit. Not father wit—it's called mother wit because everything a child knows before it gets to school, it learns from its mother, not its father. And if it never goes to school, whatever native intelligence it has, it got it primarily from its mother, not its father; so it's called mother wit. And the mother is also the one who teaches the child how to speak its language, so that the natural tongue is called the mother tongue. Whenever you find as many people as we who aren't able to speak any mother tongue, why, that's evidence right there something was done to our mother. Something had to have happened to her.

They had laws in those days that made it mandatory for a Black child to be taken from its mother as fast as that child was born. The mother never had a chance to rear it. The child would be brought up somewhere else away from the mother, so that the mother couldn't teach the child what she knewCabout itself, about her past, about its heritage. It would have to grow up in complete darkness, knowing nothing about the land it came from or the people that it came from. Not even about its own mother. There was no relationship between the Black child and its mother; it was against the law. And if the master would ever find any of those children who had any knowledge of its mother tongue, that child was put to death. They had to stamp out the language; they did it scientifically. If they found any one of them that could speak it, off went its head, or they would put it to death, they would kill it, in front of the mother, if necessary. This is history; this is how they took your language. You didn't lose it, it didn't evaporate they took it with a scientific process, because they knew they had to take it to make you dumb, or into the dummy that you and I now are.

I read in some books where it said that some of the slave mothers would try and get tricky. In order to teach their child, who'd be off in another field somewhere, they themselves would be praying and they'd pray in a loud voice, and in their own language. The child in the distant field would hear his mother's voice, and he'd learn how to pray in the same way; and in learning how to pray, he'd pick up on some of the language. And the master found out that this was being done, and immediately he stepped up his efforts to kill all the little children that were benefitting from this. And so it became against the law even for the slave to be caught praying in his tongue, if he knew it. It was against the law. You've heard some of the people say they had to pray with their heads in a bucket. Well, they weren't praying to the Jesus that they're praying to now. The white man will let you call on that Jesus all day long; in fact he'll make it possible for you to call on him. If you were calling on that somebody else, then he'd have more fear of it. Your calling on that somebody else in that other language—that causes him a bit of fear, a bit of freight.

They used to have to steal away to pray. All those songs that the slaves talked, or sang, and called spirituals, had wrapped up in them some of what was happening to them. And when the child realized that it couldn't hear its mother pray anymore, the slaves would come up with a song, "I Couldn't Hear Nobody Pray," or the song "Motherless Child": "Sometimes, I feel like a motherless child. Father gone, mother gone, motherless child sees a hard time." All of these songs were describing what was happening to us then, in the only way slaves knew how to communicate—in song. They didn't dare say it outright, so they put it in song. They pretended that they were singing about Moses in "Go Down, Moses." They weren't talking about Moses and telling "old Pharaoh to let my people go." They were trying to talk some kind of talk to each other, over the slave master's head. Now you've got a hold of the thing and you're believing in it for real. Yes, I hear you singing "Go down, Moses," and you're still talking about Moses four thousand years ago—you're out of your mind. But those slaves had a whole lot of sense. Everything they sang was designed toward freedom. ...

In making the case that Ebonics is good, the rest of this book is divided into nine chapters. Chapter one introduces the Ebonics issue. Chapter two examines the linguistic reality of African American English. Chapter three looks at the sociolinguistics of African American English. Chapter four focuses on the politico-sociolinguistic reality of African American English. Chapter five discusses the social construction of Ebonics from a Fasoldian perspective. Chapter six is about the Oakland Unified School District (OUSD) initiative. Chapter seven presents the linguistic connections between the African National Anthem (Nkosi Sikelel'i Afrika), the Jamaican National Anthem (Jamaica), and the Negro National Anthem (Lift Ev'ry Voice and Sing). Chapter eight entails the conclusion and suggestion. And Chapter nine offers a couple of reflections. Together, these chapters demonstrate that a thorough description of African American English (AAE) requires that we locate its total personality within the boundaries of its own self-perception. This means that we must delineate AAE and its view of the world, both visible and invisible, its fundamental habits of thought, and its attitude towards its physical and spiritual existence.

The roots of the African American life concept is holistic: that is, it is based on an integrative world view. All life to the African is total; all human activities are closely interrelated. This has as its underlying principle the sanctity of the person, his/her spirituality and essentiality. This essentialist view of the person confers value to his/her personhood. All else—his/her labor and achievements—flow from this value system. Even personal failure cannot invalidate it.

Indeed, no book can be all things to all readers. My guess is that what follows will strike a responsive chord in some and leave others quite untouched; this is preferable to a wide, but tepid, acceptance.

CHAPTER 1

☩

INTRODUCTION

What an animal kingdom we now find ourselves, where some are more equal than others and vultures and hyenas consider themselves kahunas and could summon the courage to call brave Lions jackals.

—Sami Gandy-Gorgla, 2005

In the wake of the Oakland, California, school board's declaration in December of 1996 that African American English, also known as Ebonics (a term coined from two words, ebony and phonics, by African American psychologist Robert Williams in 1975), is not merely a dialect but a language, rooted in a distinct African American culture, and that students who speak it should not be criticized or harshly corrected, but given special assistance learning standard English. A number of White and African American public figures jumped into the discussion of the issue, about which they were not well informed. As reported in the Washington Post (December 25, 1996, p. A2), U.S. Department of Education secretary Richard W. Riley, speaking on behalf of the Clinton administration, stated that "Elevating 'black English' to the status of a language is not the way to raise standards of achievement in our schools and for our students." The Rev. Jesse L. Jackson said that "I understand the attempt to reach out to these children, but this is an unacceptable surrender border lining on disgrace." On NBC's Meet the Press, Jackson added that "It's teaching down to our children and it must never happen." California governor Pete Wilson (Republican) was no more encouraging of Oakland's experiment than Clinton. Wilson's press secretary, Sean Walsh, asserted that "The mainstreaming of this ridiculous theory (Ebonics) will only serve to hold [disadvantaged children] back." The presupposition of these statements is that African American English is a "bad" language. What I attempt to demonstrate in this book, as I stated earlier, is that African American English is a GOOD language because it possesses the dual character any other language has: it is both a means of communication and a carrier of culture. Accordingly, as Robert Williams defines it in the book he edited and appropriately titled Ebonics: The True Language of Black Folk (1975), Ebonics refers to "the linguistic and paralinguistic features which on a concentric continuum represents the communicative competence of the West African, Caribbean, and United States idioms (usual ways in which words of a particular language are joined together to express thought), patois (a form of language differing generally from the accepted standard), argots (specialized vocabularies and idioms of groups), idiolects (dialects of individuals), and social forces of Black people. Ebonics derives its form from ebony (Black) and phonics (sound, the study of sound) and refers to the study of the language of Black people in all its cultural uniqueness" (1975:vi, the definitions in parentheses are added by me).

Challenging the devaluation of African American English is important because of the devastating consequences that may result from such an action. Language can take a people further and further from themselves to other selves, from their world to other worlds.

The biblical account of the people of Gilead in about 1100 B.C. records that they had killed a number of Ephraimites and then devised a linguistic discrimination test to flush out the remaining enemy in the land. In the book of Judges, we read:

> ...The men of Gilead said to them, "Are you Ephraimites?" If they answered "no,"
> they then asked them, "Say the word Shibboleth." The true Ephraimites responded,
> "Sibboleth," for they could not pronounce it right (*Judges* 12:5,6).

Also, as Charles Barron, a citizen of Gullah country and an affiliate of the Dynamics of Leadership, Inc., in New York, reminds us, on June 16, 1976, in Soweto, South Africa, African students organized an uprising to protest the teaching of Afrikaans, the language of the White, racist oppressors, in their schools. For the Afrikaaners, it was so important that their language be taught that they ordered their army to massacre over one thousand African youth. The South African White oppressors, bent on maintaining their demonic system of apartheid in order to dominate for generations to come, forced their language on the African youth.

In addition, as Ngũgĩ wa Thiong'o recounts in one of his outstanding books, *Decolonising the Mind* (1981), one of the most humiliating experiences in colonial Kenya was to be caught speaking Gĩkũyũ in the vicinity of Thiong'o's school. The culprit was given corporal punishment—three to five strokes of the cane on bare buttocks—or was made to carry a metal plate around the neck with inscriptions such as I AM STUPID or I AM A DONKEY. The teachers caught culprits by giving a button to one student who was supposed to hand it over to whomever was caught speaking his/her mother tongue. Whoever had the button at the end of the day would sing the name of the student who had given it to him or her, and the ensuing process would bring out all the culprits of the day. Thus, students were turned into witch-hunters, and in the process were being taught the lucrative value of being traitors to their immediate community.

In colonial Africa, the system of education, in addition to its apartheid racial demarcation, had the structure of a pyramid: a broad primary base, a narrowing secondary middle, and an even narrower university apex. Selections from primary into secondary, and from secondary into university, were through rigorous public examinations, in which one had to pass six subjects ranging from math to the physical sciences and a European language. All the papers were written in a European language. Anyone who failed the European language could not pass the exams, no matter how brilliantly she or he had done in the other subjects. One can have distinctions in the physical sciences and math and a simple pass in English, but will not be admitted into a university. Instead, one needs to pass the European language with at least a credit (equivalent to a grade of "B" in the American educational system) to gain admission.

But obviously it was worse, according to Ngég« wa Thiong'o, when the colonial child was exposed to images of his or her world as mirrored in the written languages of the colonizer. In the child's own impressionable mind, African languages were associated in his/her impressionable mind with low status, humiliation, corporal punishment, slow-footed intelligence and ability or downright stupidity, no intelligence, and barbarism. This was reinforced by the world encountered in the works of such racists as a Rider Haggard or a Nicholas Monsarrat, not to mention the pronouncements of some of the giants of Western intellectual and political establishments, such as Hume ("… the negro is naturally inferior to the whites …"), Thomas Jefferson ("… the blacks … are inferior to the whites on the endowments of both body and mind …"), or Hegel, with his comparison of Africa to a land of childhood still enveloped in the dark mantle of the night, as far as the development of self-conscious history was concerned. Hegel's statement that there was nothing harmonious with humanity to be found in the African character is representative of the racist images of Africans and Africa such a colonial child was bound to encounter in the literature of the colonial languages. The results could be disastrous, as is the case of African Americans who have always been ostracized (deliberate exclusion of an individual or group from society) for their language.

After the attacks on the World Trade Center in New York and the Pentagon in Washington, D.C., on September 11, 2001, nearly the entire world was outraged by the acts, and correctly so, for those acts must be labeled what they are: terrorist acts that have no basis in Islam. And also correctly so, the area of the attack in the heart of New York's financial district has become a monument for America's resolve. We must also not forget the history of that financial district. It is an area where thousands of native first Americans and Africans were butchered by European Americans for their selfish gains.

Between 1640 and 1645, the Manhattan, an indigenous people of North America of the Algonquian-Wakashan linguistic group belonging to the Wappinger Confederacy, were brutally wiped out by the Dutch. The Wappinger, who are said to have sold Manhattan to the Dutch for a handful of beads and trinkets (legendarily valued at $24) on May 24, 1626, objected to the idea that they sold their land, because what they understood they did was accept rental payment for use of a particular portion of Manhattan Island as a trading center, so they could do business with the Dutch. And Peter Minuit, the director of the Dutch colony, born in Wesel, Duchy of

Cleves (present-day Germany), knew fully well that this had not been a sale, but rather a rental. Minuit resolved the issue by sending a military expedition up the island to dispense with the Wappinger. The expedition did, so rapidly that Minuit's troops felt no one would believe how successful they had been when they went back—so they took the heads of the fighting-age males and the leaders, and carried them back in woven baskets to display as proof that they had butchered the lot. The citizenry was so happy that they gathered around to watch a jolly sporting contest of soccer and football, in which the heads of the slain owners of the land were used as soccer balls or footballs. It is roughly on that place where the foundation of the World Trade Center is situated.

Anyone familiar with Native/First American culture knows that the Wappinger were correct in their linguistic interpretation of the deal. The Dutch simply engaged in linguistic manipulation for their own selfish economic, political and social gains. Selling land is not a Native/First American custom. Land is to be used and allowed to re-fertilize itself by moving elsewhere so as not to destroy it. For the Native/First American, land is owned by the Creator, not man.

The actions of the Dutch killed more than just a people; they also killed the Wappinger language. It is just one example of thousands of native first American language deaths that have been caused by European Americans. Some scholars estimate that at the time of the first European contact, the western hemisphere was inhabited by 40 million people who spoke 1,800 different languages. Another widely accepted estimate suggests that at the time of Columbus, more than 15 million speakers throughout that half of the world used more than 2,000 languages. By the end of the 20th century, as a result of European conquest and settlement in the western hemisphere, perhaps two-thirds of the many indigenous American languages had been killed. Of the native first American languages still in use, more than half are spoken by fewer than 1,000 persons per language; most of the speakers are bilingual. Only a few languages, like Navajo and Cherokee, have more than 50,000 speakers; Navajo, spoken by about 150,000 people, is the most widely used native first American language in the United States. By the end of the 20th century, 175 native American languages were spoken in the United States, but only 20 of these were widely known, and 55 were spoken by only a few elderly members; 100 other languages were somewhere between these extremes.

The same financial district sits on an area where enslaved Africans were butchered and an African burial ground is situated. Wall Street itself got its name from the wall of a protective slave enclosure, which formed the economy of the city, which is now considered the economic head of an empire.

On April 7, 1712, over 20 enslaved Africans, hoping to incite other Africans, gathered in an orchard on Maiden Lane to revolt against British rule. (The British were much more ruthless than the Dutch, passing 36 laws restricting the Africans. This was the first organized slave revolt in New York. During the melee, the house of Peter van Tilburgh was burned, and nine members of his household and neighboring homes were killed. The rebels escaped into the forest, but the governor posted sentries at all spots where the enslaved could leave the island of Manhattan, such as the ferry slip to Brooklyn or the Harlem River Bridge, making it impossible for them to leave the area. The British found all of them the next day, although six had committed suicide rather than face the torture and execution by the British. Those captured were burned alive over a slow fire for eight to ten hours, dragged through the streets behind a cart, and lashed at every corner as a warning to anyone else who wanted freedom. Twenty-one Africans were brutally executed, including some who had their insides gored out. These enslaved Africans are among those buried in New York City's African Burial Ground at Duane Street.

In October 2003, a group of anthropologists and archeologists determined that one grave contained a young woman who had twisted, snapped wrists and a bullet lodged in her ribs. In another was a man laid to rest with coins on his eyes, an African custom. A third grave site at the colonial-era burial ground had a woman holding a child in her arms. Researchers believe that the burial ground, which was closed in 1794, is part of a larger one that stretches five blocks and is encircled by the State Supreme Court, the federal Courthouse, and City Hall. It is thought that 20,000 Africans are buried there some historians believe this proves that a much larger African population lived in New York during the 18th century than originally estimated.

Scores of artifacts found in the coffins—waist beads, cowrie shells, necklaces, bracelets, and small pieces of pottery—were examined by a team of the nation's top anthropologists and archeologists at Howard University, which conducted the bio-skeletal research of the site. These scientists believe that many of those buried in the grave site were born in Africa rather than in North America. They have matched DNA samples of people from Ghana and the Ivory Coast to some of the remains. Some of the dead suffered from tropical diseases they could have contracted only in the Caribbean or in other warmer climates. At least 18 of the skeletal remains contained teeth that had been filed in the same designs seen only in Africa.

For the scientists, that meant the enslaved Africans were treated badly. The face of the woman with the bullet lodged in her side had been smashed. They also found that at least 70 percent of the adults suffered a condition where the muscles along the neck area are detached. Such a condition is usually seen in weight lifters or people who consistently carry loads too heavy for them.

The ostracism of African Americans by the majority of White Americans has been going on for approximately 400 years. The ostracism has had some long-lasting devastating consequences in terms of what is referred to as *semantic-information distance*—the gap in information and understanding that exists between superior and subordinates, or other groups within an organization, on specified issues (Jablin et al. 1979:1207). The gap in information and understanding between African Americans and Whites continues to exist. It has been handed over from one generation to another and, therefore, has become cultural in a sense. This has led to what communication experts call "definitional physical interdependence." From the time the Africans were brought to this country as enslaved people, there was little interaction between them and their White masters. So, it was extremely difficult for African Americans to learn Standard American English. This, of course, is the major exigency for Ebonics.

For a language to be both learned and shared, it must be transmitted from one member of a group to another in some ways. This process is normally called socialization, which tends to be both formal and informal (the informal part of the process being spontaneous). Without social-ization, a group's culture could not be transmitted to its new members (Bluedom 1995:501). One views culture broadly as a social heritage that is passed on and modified from one genera-tion to another. A system of agreed-upon meanings that serve as guidelines for behavior in any particular society also encompasses what the group has learned, created, and done to guarantee its biological survival through time (Keto 1991:2). This is another reason African Americans developed Ebonics. As culture and language are interrelated, this was how African Americans developed a subculture and language based on their ostracism.

From a variety of data sources, the effects of the ostracism of African Americans by many White Americans are quite evident. First, African Americans are overrepresented in all dis-ability categories. Second, it is the group most likely to be placed in segregated classrooms or buildings. Finally, the patterns of language learning and usage of African Americans are generally devalued in schools. But as Heath's classic ethnographic study of African American and White children's language learning demonstrates, these children learn spontaneously with their peers how to talk in the imaginative, playful, and performing mode of "talking junk," with the boys becoming particularly competitive in the skill (Harry and Anderson 1994). So, it appears that despite the ostracism, one reality remains: Ebonics will not gradually fade off into the night. It is part of the foundation of African American identity; and whether people want to admit it or not, it is a part of American culture.

Nonetheless, another disturbing implication of this pattern of ostracism is that African Americans are more likely to be educated in separate schools that will prepare them for separate and even more punitive facilities when they leave school than for the real world of work and responsibility. The more separate the educational placement, the more unrealistic and inap-propriate the instruction is likely to be, and the less preparation for real life. As Harry and Anderson (1994) point out, if a small fraction (6 percent) teenaged African American males who enter special education programs are likely to return to regular education, the implications for post-school employment, higher education, preparation for jobs that offer opportunities in high-demand technology fields, and ultimately the ability to become a source of support for their families and assume the role of responsible fatherhood are dramatically diminished.

This is a particularly sensitive issue in Oakland where, although 53 percent of the District's 51,000 students are African American, they account for 64 percent of those held back, 71 percent of those in special education programs, and 80 percent of those suspended. Almost 20 percent of these African Americans in grade 12 do not graduate (*USA Today* 1997:12A).

In the Baltimore, whose public school student population is 80 percent African American, 18 percent of all students were placed in special education programs in 1988 (Maryland State Department of Education 1988). The way special education is currently conceptualized, this means that almost one-fifth of the students in that city were designated as disabled for educa-tional purposes. This is clearly counterproductive and suggests that the entire system needs to be reconceptualized (Harry and Anderson 1994).

As *Los Angeles Times* (March 24, 2005) writer Duke Helfand reports, a recent Harvard University study reveals that nearly half of the Latino and African American students who should have graduated from California's high schools in 2002 did not. Statewide, just 57 percent of African Americans and 60 percent of Latinos graduated in 2002, compared with 78 percent of Whites and 84 percent of Asians. In the Los Angeles Unified School District, the situation was even worse, with just 39 percent of Latinos and 47 percent African Americans graduating, compared with 67 percent of Whites and 77 percent of Asians. The study concluded that the public is largely unaware of the true extent of the problem, as the state uses "misleading and inaccurate" methods to report dropout and graduation rates. The California Department of Education reported that 87 percent of students graduated in 2002, but the Harvard researchers pegged the rate at 71 percent.

According to Helfand, the troubling graduation rates in the minority communities is due to the fact that these are places where students are more likely to attend what researchers call "dropout factories." The exodus of thousands of students before 12th grade is exacting significant social and economic costs through higher unemployment, increased crime, and billions of dollars in lost revenue. Jefferson High School principal Norm Morrow is cited as attributing his school's graduation rate partly to a transient student population and overcrowding, which leave little opportunity for personal attention. He is also quoted as saying that "If you don't connect with [students], they are going to drop out."

CHAPTER 2

LINGUISTIC REALITY OF AFRICAN AMERICAN ENGLISH

African American linguist Charles DeBose (1991) suggests that in the 1960s, African American English became a hot topic in linguistics. Many of the earlier works labeled it Negro dialect, or nonstandard Negro English, but the term Black English eventually became the generic technical term employed by linguists. For the general public, it remained novel and controversial to suggest that the language in question was anything but "bad" English; and among informed African Americans, there were strong feelings for or against various alternative terms, including Ebonics. Nobody asked the average sister or brother on the street what this language should be called, but I suspect that if anyone had, the answer would have been "English"—plain and simple.

When I speak of English grammar from an African-centric perspective, I am talking about the perspective of the sisters and brothers in everyday walks of life. Such is the perspective of my research on African American linguistics. The African-centric perspective is not adequately represented in the body of linguistic knowledge that has grown out of the academic study of the English of African Americans. The definition of "Black English" within that tradition is a case study of the extent to which the sociocultural perspective from which academic work is conducted can shape, color, and ultimately determine its directions, priorities, basic assumptions, and applications to broader societal concerns.

From an African-centric perspective, the English of African Americans is normal and acceptable. In my book in progress, *Linguistic Connections Between African* and *African American Languages*, I demonstrate that the linguistic features that define the Eurocentric notion of Black English conform to African American cultural norms, and reflect the continuation of linguistic patterns common to the languages of West and Central Africa. African American English sounds fine to us Black folk, and deep down inside we don't know what the problem is when the English teacher tries to correct our verbs. We know you *ain't* supposed to say *ain't*, and we know you should say *you are*, and not *you is*, although we relax and forget sometimes. Actually, deep down inside, *you is* sounds better sometimes, as in the case of the brother who says "Baby/(Mama), you sho is fine" (DeBose 1991:1).

When I studied linguistics and came into a scientific awareness of language, I realized that we had been correct all along in our deep-down feelings about our "you ises" being okay, and that those teachers had been wrong in their attempts to correct us. This is a radical position, I know, but it is squarely in line with the axiomatic principles of descriptive linguistics. All human languages, not only standard written varieties, but also dialects, vernaculars, and creoles, are systematic and rule-governed. The traditional devaluation of the English of African Americans, thus, is at odds with universally accepted linguistic principles.

In linguistics we make a distinction between rules of grammar, or descriptive rules, on the one hand, and rules of usage, or prescriptive rules, on the other hand. Rules of grammar account for the language that we produce spontaneously, from deep down inside, without hardly giving it a thought. Rules of usage account for the language we are taught to produce, and should produce, in order to please the English teacher. From the purely descriptive point of view, *Baby/(Mama), you sho is fine* is just as grammatical as *Dear, you certainly are attractive*. The clause *you sho is fine* is syntactically well-formed in that it contains a subject in the form of the pronoun *you*, a predicate headed by the copula verb *is* preceded by the adverbial intensifier *sho*, and this is followed by the predicate adjective *fine* (DeBose 1991:2).

Besides, as I have argued elsewhere (Bangura 1990:4), it may seem that no such object as language exists, or that its invention is more ingenious than useful. This is because the only "language" real people encounter is something like a variety of Mandingo or a variety of English, etc. Language that is not a language is obviously an abstraction. But even "English" is not found in the concrete, and no one has ever spoken it. In order to speak "English," one would have to simultaneously speak cockney and all the other British dialects, to talk at the same time just like Irish, Nigerian, Sierra Leonean, Scottish, Canadian, Indian, Australian, Filipino, South African, American, etc.—speakers whose native language is "English." That these speakers have no trouble understanding books the others write, and that most can grasp what the others say (given a bit of time!) would suggest that there is something about "English" that is not identical with its concrete manifestations.

What I am claiming then is that the notion of 'Black English' is not an Africancentric concept. Rather, I would argue, it is a cover term for the linguistic ethnicity of Black people. When the traits by which a people are identified are viewed from the perspective of outsiders, they are seen as ethnicity. Attention is drawn to those very traits which differ markedly from corresponding traits of the outsiders; be they physical traits such as skin color and hair texture, or cultural traits such as language. When white Americans hear African Americans speaking English, their attention is drawn to particular features which contrast markedly with their English: the absence of the copula (e.g., *How you doing?*), the simplification of final consonant clusters (e.g., *It's Henry eatin.*), the use of be as an uninflected verb (e.g., *We be playing ball.*), the use of the logical variability of the -*s* in the third-person singular (e.g., *She see them.*), the use of question inversion and 'existential it' (e.g., *It's a man at the door?*), the employment of the 'negativized auxiliary preposition' (e.g., *Don't nobody know nothing?*), etc. (for more features, see the three articles by Hoover et al. in Jones, ed. 1996). Much of the existing literature on Black English consists of studies of such features: i.e. of linguistic ethnicity.

We gain insight into the essence of the African American English phenomenon by considering the fact that there are predictable reactions to ethnicity, the most obvious of which is humor, fascination, and dread. The success of the popular 1950s television show Amos 'n Andy exemplifies the predictably humorous reaction likely invoked by a stereotypical imitation of African American language is likely to evoke. When historically black colleges and universities (HBCUs) utilize their marching bands and choruses in effective fund-raising efforts, their success may be seen as a predictable reaction to ethnicity in the form of fascination with African American music. A good example of the dreaded African American ethnicity sometimes elicits is the effectiveness of the notorious "Willie Horton" commercials used by George Bush during the 1988 presidential campaign (DeBose 1991:2).

There are less obvious but still predictable reactions to ethnicity, and only two will be mentioned here: self-hate and cultural appropriation. As an example of self-hate, consider the use of the term "bad hair" by a curly-haired person in reference to that type of hair. Or consider the designation of language replete with you ises as "bad English" by someone who says "you is." As an example of cultural appropriation, consider the emergence of rock music through the performance of African American rhythm and blues material by White artists such as Elvis Presley, the Beatles, or Michael Bolton (DeBose 1991:3).

The major contributors to the academic field of Black English (e.g., William Labov and John Dillard) might themselves be seen as engaging in cultural appropriation, as they capitalize upon the fascination and humor of ethnic language to add zest to their lectures and intrigue to their theoretical positions, not to ignore their academic tenures and speaking honoraria. The ethnicity orientation of Eurocentric Black English Studies focuses attention upon the social stigma traditionally associated with stereotypical notions of Black folk speech, and has stimulated emotionally charged, and largely uninformed, debate on the educational policy implications of African American language (DeBose 1991:3).

What has been conspicuously missing in the musings of Ebonics' opponents is the recognition of the connections between Ebonics and some languages in Africa. This is not accidental, as the debate over the linguistic connections between African and African American languages has been controversial since Melville J. Herskovits's pioneering work was published in 1941. The debate was heightened when E. Franklin Frazier's work was published in 1963. While Herskovits proposed that African linguistic features have survived in North America and have been retained by a process of acculturation and adaptation, Frazier emphasized African linguistic discontinuity and advocated a deculturalization hypothesis.

While Herskovits's work was pioneering in allowing detailed analysis of the linguistic connections between African and African American languages, it nonetheless was limited because it was based entirely on the West African zones. Following Herskovits, Whitten and Szwed (1970), Bastide (1971), Mintz (1974), Mintz and Price (1976), Levine (1977), Moreno Fraginals (1984), and Asante (1990) implicitly suggest a West African baseline for the linguistic connections. However, Wood (1974), Vass (1979), Stuckey (1987), and Holloway (1990) revise Herskovits' baseline to include Bantu origin for many facets of the linguistic connections. Holloway and Vass (1993) use two cultural baselines to assess the linguistic connections: a West African baseline and a Central African baseline.

In addition, a number of dictionaries and related works which provide documentation of linguistic connections between African and African American languages. The most comprehensive of these works is from Turner (1949). His dictionary provides an extensive documentation of Africanisms in the speech of African Americans. It has approximately 5,000 words that originated in West and Central Africa.

Gold (1960) traces the history and origin of jazz to the old Congo Square in New Orleans, one of the North American Bantu culture centers. The word *jazz* is derived from *jaja*, meaning "to make or cause to dance." The Bantu root for "dance" is *ja*. *Jaja*, a doubling of the verb root, is the causative form of the verb. Thus, jazz was music to which people could dance (Holloway and Vass 1993:xvi). Gold reveals how African Americans used "jive talk," a coded language with African words, during slavery to communicate a double entendre designed to conceal meanings from Whites. Gold provides a list of important linguistic Africanisms that formed part of African American English in the 1930s, 1940s, and 1950s.

Dalby (1972) provides a dictionary of linguistic Africanisms from Wolof found in Standard American English and African American English. Dalby identifies early African linguistic retentions of Wolof-Mande origins and traced them back to Africa.'

Dalgish (1972) provides a list of African-derived words and phrases used in English. The shortcoming in Dalgish's work is that the definition of Africanism hinges on African words cited in European and African publications. These words are inadequate to serve as the basis for Africanisms, since Africanism, by definition, is any cultural (material or nonmaterial) or linguistic property of African origin surviving in the New World or in the African diaspora.

Dillard's first work (1975) is on the impact of pidgins (formed when two cultures first come into contact) and creoles (established when the pidgin becomes the mother tongue of the following generation) on Standard American English. Dillard shows how some Africanisms became Americanized. Dillard's second work (1976) looks at Africanisms in African American naming practices: personal names, jazz, blues, church names, vehicle names, shops, vendors, and things for sale. Dillard shows that Africanisms in African American naming practices are not unique to African Americans, but that they are also used by Whites. Dillard's third work (1977) examines Ebonics. It is a dictionary of African American English used over time by African Americans. The major hypothesis in this work is that language used among African Americans derives from a complex set of cultural transparencies and is maintained by an equally complex set of social and communication networks. Dillard concludes, however, that African American vernacular survived from Africa in new structural linguistic forms.

Puckett's (1975) collection of African names in America is a comprehensive source of African American personal names, providing information on words of African origin and meanings with possible ethnic group and gender identification. Of the approximately 500,000 names listed by Puckett, 340,000 are used by African Americans and 160,000 are used by Whites. According to Puckett, both enslaved and free African Americans identified strongly with their African culture and heritage, as demonstrated in the retention of African personal names and naming practices. Fewer of these names were in popular use by African Americans by the middle of the 19th Century as a direct result of pressures from White Americans for African Americans to conform to western European traditions and practices.

Smitherman (1977) provides a list of African American English and African-derived words found in Standard American English. Smitherman examines words of direct African origin, gives special attention to African words surviving in Standard American English, and looks at loan translations from Africa found exclusively in African American English. Thus, Smitherman concludes that African American languages are deeply based in an African linguistic structure reflecting an African heritage, meaning, and gesture.

Major (1978) provides a dictionary of words credited to and used by African Americans. Each word is defined, and its date and geographical areas of usage are identified. The major tenor of this work is that African American English is deeply based in African linguistic retention.

Cassidy and LePage (1980) offer a comprehensive list of words in everyday Jamaican English. They also cross-list a few Africanisms in North America within the context of Jamaican English.

Holm and Shilling (1982) offer a comprehensive list of words in Bahamian English, which forms an important link between Caribbean English and Gullah, the African American English variety spoken in coastal communities from northern Florida to North Carolina. The connections between Bahamian English and Gullah present an excellent perspective for the study of African American English in the United States.

Miller and Smith (1989) present an extensive glossary of Harlem speech, in which a large number of Africanisms exist. The focus of this work is on African Americans in the United States, starting with their "first" arrival in Jamestown.

Keller (1989) provides nearly 800 entries of a wide range of information on personalities, places, and events that relate to African American aesthetics and politics. The focus of the work is on the Harlem Renaissance.

Goss and Barnes (1989) present an anthology of African American storytelling brought into the Americas by African captives. These authors show that the art form has remained largely dormant among descendants of the original captives except in family and church meetings. They note, however, that the art is now being resurrected, primarily through the work of pioneering giants in the profession, such as Brother Blue (Hugh Morgan Hill, PhD), Mary Carter Smith, and Jackie Torrence. In the past, Goss and Barnes point out, these storytellers have gone by many names. Today, they are called preachers, healers, teachers, comedians, blues singers, poets, dancers, rappers, liars, painters, and historians. To see them tell the story is to experience highlights of African ritual—at its best, a total theatrical performance.

What all these works demonstrate is that the almost total absence of visible African artifacts in African American culture does not warrant the view that nothing African survived the tyranny of American slavery. While the visible artifacts of religious sculpture gradually disappeared, subtler linguistic and communicative artifacts were sustained and embellished by the Africans' creativity.

CHAPTER 3

✝

SOCIOLINGUISTICS OF AFRICAN AMERICAN ENGLISH

The name African American English (AAE) is a cover term employed by linguists. It refers to a continuum of varieties whose features may be very similar to or very different from those of Standard American English (SAE) (depending on which end of the continuum one considers). The name African American English is used to acknowledge the fact that these varieties are spoken primarily by and among African Americans. Nonetheless, it is imperative to note that not all African Americans are speakers of AAE and that others besides African Americans speak the language. Indeed, spoken language is not in any way predestined, but is instead determined by exposure to the language. So just as a person born in New York does not automatically become a speaker of New York English, an African American is not predestined to become a speaker of AAE. Similarly, a member of a different ethnic group who is exposed to AAE as a first language will likely become a speaker of AAE.

While these varieties are defined in terms of ethnicity, other demographic variables such as age, area of residence, gender, socioeconomic status, and style can influence AAE varieties, as they do other language varieties. An 80-year-old African American speaker of AAE will speak differently from a 14-year-old AAE speaker. A male AAE speaker will likely have different features in his speech than a female AAE speaker. An AAE speaker from California will speak differently from an AAE speaker from Texas. And it is likely that a middle-class AAE speaker will have different features compared to a working-class AAE speaker. Moreover, no individual speaker of AAE speaks the same way all the time. Instead, one varies her or his speech depending on style and context.

THE ORIGIN OF AFRICAN AMERICAN ENGLISH

The origin of AAE has been an issue of great debate among linguists. The debate hinges upon two theories: the dialectologist and the Creolist. A unified perspective has also emerged out of these two theories. These views are described in the following three subsections.

THE DIALECTOLOGIST THEORY

The dialectologist school of thought posits that AAE traces its roots back to the varieties of English spoken in the British Isles, just like other regional varieties of American English. Beginning around the 1920s and continuing into the 1940s, dialectologists presented the first scholarly analyses of African American English, arguing that AAE should be analyzed in terms of regional differences, just like any other variety of English (see Figure 1). Essentially, it was believed that African Americans spoke the language of European Americans with whom they shared comparable socio-economic and regional backgrounds. AAE was believed to have originated as a southern variety of English, which spread northward during the 1920s migration of African Americans of the South and into northern cities, because of the decline of the cotton industry and the growing job opportunities in the industrial North. Varieties of southern English spoken by African Americans in areas such as Alabama, Georgia, Mississippi, and South Carolina were, therefore, spread northward into Chicago, Detroit, New York, Philadelphia, and Washington, D.C. (Whether Washington, D.C., is a northern territory is another matter). This migration was said to account for the fact that, unlike other regional varieties of English, certain features of AAE exhibited a sort of "supraregional homogeneity."

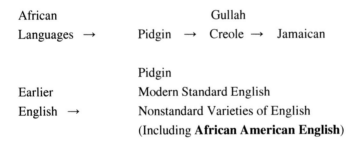

Figure 1: The Dialectologist Hypothesis

THE CREOLIST THEORY

The Creolists challenge the dialectologists by arguing that AAE traces its roots back to the times of the slave trade when West Africans from regions such as Ghana, The Gambia, Guinea, Ivory Coast, Mali, Nigeria, Senegal, and Sierra Leone were forced together on slave ships with no common language among them. They were exposed to many different African languages, such as Bulu, Hausa, Wolof, and Twi, as well as the English of the ships' sailors (see Figure 2).

In most instances, enslaved Africans were isolated from speakers of their own native languages in order to avoid possible uprisings. Consequently, enslaved Africans were forced to develop some common form of communication.

Out of this language contact emerged a Pidgin language—i.e., a speech system that is formed to provide a means of communication between people who do not share a common language. As the enslaved Africans formed communities on the slave plantations of the southeast Atlantic seaboard, this Pidgin became the primary means of communication for many of the enslaved. When a pidgin becomes the principal language of a speech community, it is referred to as a creole. According to Creolists, increased contact between speakers of this creole and speakers of other English varieties resulted in the decreolization (change in a creole that makes it more like the standard language of a territory) of this language, which has led to the present-day AAE.

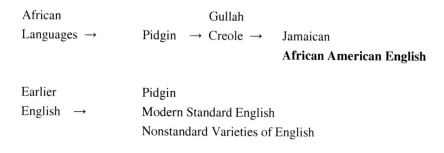

Figure 2: The Creolist Hypothesis

To support their theory, Creolists analyze features found in AAE that resemble English-based creoles of the Caribbean, such as Jamaican Creole or creoles of Africa, such as Krio spoken in Sierra Leone. The only surviving English-based creole in the United States is Gullah, which is spoken primarily in the southeastern regions of South Carolina. Many Creolists today regard Gullah to be a direct link to the origins of AAE, believing it to resemble the creole ancestor of AAE.

THE UNIFIED PERSPECTIVE

For many years, linguists were radically divided between the dialectologist and Creolist theories concerning the roots of AAE. The issue remains unresolved to this day. However, it appears that movement is being made toward an understanding of AAE that accepts some reasoning from both schools of thought (see Figure 3). Put differently, proponents of the unified view believe that the dialectologist and Creolist positions may not be mutually exclusive, but instead both may contribute to the understanding of the origins, history, and development of AAE in the United States.

```
                        Modern Standard English
African                 Gullah
Languages →    Pidgin  → Creole →   Jamaican, etc.
                        African American English


          Pidgin
Earlier   Jamaican
English  → Gullah
          Modern Standard English
          Nonstandard Varieties of English →      Other Varieties
                                                  African
                                                  American
                                                  English
```

Figure 3: The Unified Approach

SALIENT LINGUISTIC FEATURES OF AFRICAN AMERICAN ENGLISH

The salient linguistic features of AAE can be classified into the following categories:

Phonological Features: (1) consonant cluster simplification or reduction, (2) final consonant simplification or deletion, (3) final and post-vocalic -*r* variation, (4) [ω] + [n] realized as [æ] and [ω] + [nk] realized as [ænk], (5) [θ] ' [f] in word/syllable-final position, (6) [ð] ' [d] in word/syllable-initial position, (7) [ð] ' [v] in word/syllable-medial position, and (8) -l deletion or reduction in word/syllable-medial or word/syllable-final position.

Morphological Features: (1) suffix -*s* variation—plural -*s* (contextual signals), possessive -*s* (contextual signals), third-person singular -*s*, and reduplicated -*s* or reinterpretation of -*s*; and (2) past tense markers.

Syntactic Features: (1) copula deletion or variation, (2) they possessive, (3) it expletive, (4) gon, (5) multiple negation, (6) aspectual verb -*s* suffix, (7) pronominal apposition, (8) perfective or completive done, (9) stressed or remotive been, (10) aspectual or immutable been, (11) future be, (12) future perfective be done, and (13) aspectual steady.

Lexical Features: Words.

To illustrate the systemization of AAE as a rule-governed system, a sample of these features are presented as characteristic of AAE varieties. One must be reminded that not all varieties of AAE or all speakers of AAE will exhibit all of these features at all times. Many of the features or processes presented in the following subsections are discussed in relation to their SAE counterparts, not as examples of "right" versus "wrong" (since no such thing exists linguistically), but as descriptive comparisons of the two systems.

MONOPHTHONGIZATION

In AAE, a phonological process exists by which dipthongs get reduced to monophthongs word-finally or before voiced consonants.

cow [ca]
hide [had]
time [tVam]

Monophthongization before voiceless consonants is found much less frequently in AAE, albeit it may be characteristic of some southern varieties.

like [laωk] or [lak]
bite [bVaωt] or [bVat]

WORD-FINAL CONSONANT CLUSTER REDUCTION

In AAE, there exists a process of word-final consonant cluster reduction when the following word begins with a consonant. This process also exists in SAE varieties.

best buy [bɛs bʰaI]
get them [gɛ dθm]

AAE differs from SAE here, however, in that it is also possible in AAE to reduce word-final consonant clusters when the following word begins with a vowel.

cold eggs [kʰoυ egz]
best agent [bɛs egɛnt]

In English, the past tense is formed by adding a suffix, [t], [d], or [ed], given the final sound of the verb base. If the base ends in a consonant, the addition of the past tense suffix may create a consonant cluster. World-final consonant clusters that are created by the addition of the past tense suffix are also reduced in AAE.

washed my hand [waʃ maɪ han]
jumped up [jʌmp ʌp]
messed up [mɛs ʌp]

The fact that word-final past tense suffices can be deleted in these environments may give AAE the appearance of lacking a past tense suffix. However, past tense suffixes that do not form consonant clusters are not deleted by this phonological process.

painted [pentəd]
dated [detəd]

ABSENCE OF THIRD-PERSON SINGULAR SUFFIX -S

Many AAE varieties are missing the third-person singular suffix -s.

He *want* our social security to pay for his wars.
He *need* his head examined.

MULTIPLE NEGATION

In SAE, the following sentence (a) can be negated as either (b) or (c).

a. I had some pork.
b. I didn't have any pork.
c. I had no pork.

While sentences (b) and (c) may not be stylistically equivalent, they do convey the same basic meaning. The main point is that in SAE, this sentence (a) is negated by performing one of these two operations (b and c), not both. In AAE, on the other hand, it is possible to do both in the same sentence. The result is *multiple negation*, as in (d).

d. I didn't have no pork.

In fact, in AAE this operation may be performed any number of times in one sentence as in (e).

e. I don't never have no pork.

HABITUAL BE

Where SAE varieties employ adverbials such as *always* or *usually* to express habituality, AAE uses habitual *be*.

SAE	AAE
He is always lying.	He always be lying.
Sometimes she is lying, too	Sometimes she be lying, too.
She is on TV everyday lying.	She be on TV everyday lying.

The use of the uninflected *be* in the preceding AAE sentences shows that a state or activity is habitual or repeatable. Thus, *He always be lying* means that this is a recurring property of the person, as opposed to *He is lying*, which means that he has the property of lying at that particular moment. The sentence *He be lying right now* is, therefore, ungrammatical in AAE, since *be* indicates habituality, while *right now* indicates a punctual, momentary state.

Notice in SAE that if the adverbial is missing, the sentence generally loses its habitual interpretation. Compare the following two sentences:

He is *always* lying. (habitual state)
He is lying. (momentary state)

In AAE, however, uninflected *be* is itself sufficient for marking habituality, as in *He be lying* (' *He is always lying*).

LEXICAL FEATURES

Certain African words have become staples in the English language.

Word	Meaning
banjo	from Kimbundu, meaning a stringed musical instrument
bogus	from Hausa *boko*, meaning deceit or fraud
bongo	from kongo, meaning antelope
cat	suffix -kat from Wolof, denoting a person
dig	from Wolof *deg* or *dega*, meaning to understand/appreciate
wonderland	from Gola *Gondwanland*, meaning paradise on earth (the rites of passage fairy tale, "Alice in Wonderland," alludes to *Gondwanland*)
goober	from Kimbundu, meaning groundnut/peanut
Gullah	from Gola, meaning the blessing of God or the people blessed by God

gumbo	from Kimbundu, meaning okra
hip	from Wolof *hepi*, meaning to be aware of what is going on
honky	from Wolof *honq*, meaning red or pink
masa	from Bambara, meaning king, master, leader
samba	from Kongo *Quizomba*, a type of dance
tango	from Kongo, *Tangana*, a type of dance
voodoo	from Fon *vodou*, meaning spirit or family of spirits
yam	from Twi *anyiam* and Fulani *nyami* ("to eat"), edible, starchy, tuberous root
zombie	from Kongo *nzumbi*, meaning deity or fetish

CHAPTER 4

POLITICO-SOCIOLINGUISTIC REALITY OF AFRICAN AMERICAN ENGLISH

Over 200 years ago, it was recognized that African Americans spoke English differently from Whites. A British visitor writing in 1746, for example, described the American colonists this way:

> One thing they are faulty in with regard to their children...is that when young, they suffer them too much to prowl among the young Blacks, which insensibly causes them to imbibe their manners and broken speech (Trudgill 1974:58-59).0

Differences, then, were noted, and were generally held to be the result of inherent mental and physical differences between the two ethnic groups. African Americans, it was suggested, could not "speak English properly" because they were incapable of it. While this view has no basis in linguistic fact, it nevertheless persists in many circles even today, as can be noted in the debate about Ebonics. So, this book goes a step further. It assumes that there are aspects of "Language" common to any "language," and that one stage of the study of languages ought to make explicit what they are.

My contention here is that the view held by many that African American English is "inferior" is based on political rather than linguistic grounds. This proposition calls for a politico-sociolinguistic analysis of the issue. This obviously presupposes at least two major questions: (1) Why should the negative attitudes toward African American English be studied from a politico-sociolinguistic perspective? (2) What historical evidence is available to support the contention that these negative attitudes are based on political rather than linguistic grounds? These questions are sequentially examined in the following subsections.

EXAMINING NEGATIVE ATTITUDES TOWARD AFRICAN AMERICAN ENGLISH FROM A POLITICO-SOCIOLINGUISTIC PERSPECTIVE

In order to capture the plausibility and/or usefulness of examining the negative attitudes toward African American English from a politico-sociolinguistic perspective, it makes sense to begin by defining the two disciplines (Politics and Sociolinguistics) and briefly discussing their inter-relationship. This is because nothing is more natural than to study ideas in relation to other ideas. We gain knowledge through reference.

Following Trudgill (1974:13), while sociolinguistics aims to study the "relationship between language and society," politics, according to Easton (1965:51), seeks to enquire into human interactions involved in the "authoritative allocation of values"—where "values" imply desired conditions or commodities and where "authoritative" denotes some form of legitimate (i.e., governmental) processes through which people regulate their interrelationships with respect to the question of who gets what, when, and how in society. In sum, we can safely assert that both disciplines, politics and sociolinguistics, involve the study of human relationships. Indeed, a central focus on the social implications of the negative attitudes toward African American English concerns the harmonizing of the individual's needs and demands with those of society.

As Weinstein (1983:3) suggests, the relationship between language and politics is so obvious that we hardly think about it. Language is central to human society and interpersonal relations; it is the basis of civilization. Without this method of communication, Weinstein maintains, no leader could command the resources necessary for a political system extending beyond the family and neighborhood. We admit, he notes, that the ability to manipulate words in order to persuade voters is one method to obtain and hold on to power; we admire oratorical and orthographical skills as gifts, but we see no reason to treat language as a factor which is subject to conscious choices by leaders in power or by those who desire to win or to influence power. Finally, he adds, we do not think of language in terms of capital yielding measurable benefits to those who possess it.

Thus, if it can be demonstrated that African American English is the subject of policy decisions as well as a possession conferring advantages or disadvantages, a case can be made for its political analysis within the purview of sociolinguistics as one approach for understanding the debate about Ebonics. This can help us understand how African American English, as one variable, opens or closes doors to power, wealth, and prestige within the United States.

SOME HISTORICAL EVIDENCE OF POLITICALLY-MOTIVATED ATTITUDES TOWARD AFRICAN AMERICAN ENGLISH

For African Americans, their political woes, in terms of the variety of English they speak, are traceable to the 17th century, when the first group of enslaved Africans was brought to America. When these Africans arrived, they knew no English. Their usefulness as servants, however, called for some means of communication to enforce the roles of master and enslaved.

There is little likelihood that White masters exerted themselves to comprehend, much less acquire, the native languages of these early African Americans in order to communicate with them. Instead, from the very beginning White overlords addressed themselves in English to their African American vassals. The kind of English used by these overlords to their vassals was similar to that used in baby talk. It had no tenses of the verb, no distinctions of case in nouns or pronouns, no markers of singular and plural. Difficult sounds were eliminated, as they are in baby talk. Its vocabulary was reduced to the lowest possible elements. As the Africans imported to America came from many unrelated linguistic groups, speaking languages so different that one group could not understand the language of another, they were forced to employ this infantile English to communicate with one another (Turner 1949/1969:6).

Before the Civil War (1861), in an effort to keep African Americans from gaining Standard American English skills and other societal benefits, the first compulsory ignorance law was enacted by South Carolina in 1740. Many southern states followed suit. In times of slave revolts or similar insecurities, White legislators stiffened the laws, making the fines and terms of imprisonment quite stringent. The few who were caught violating the laws were actually brought to court, attesting to the almost unanimous obedience to the laws (Klingberg 1941:105).

In the 1780s, Thomas Jefferson declared African Americans to be intellectually inferior. Failing to withdraw his assertion, African Americans were, therefore, excluded from his prescriptions for American education (1968:355).

To this blatant racism, African American parents posited an equally practical opposition, not rhetorical but political. They conducted a statewide campaign in Ohio to open the schools (which their taxes helped to build) to their children; almost 15 years later, they were successful. African Americans also went on to open their own schools but would not give up their claim to the common schools. Using African American English as the medium of instruction and teaching Standard American English as a subject, these African American schools produced some of the best minds in America. As Dr. James McCune Smith, a physician and leading African American activist in New York City, declared in 1944:

> During the last 30 years, the Northern States have been the scene of a silent struggle ... the free blacks [are] taught to believe themselves naturally inferior, shut out from the temple of higher literature, and taunted with ignorance ... Freedom has strengthened our minds by throwing us upon our own resources, and has bound us to American institutions with a tenacity which nothing but death can overcome (Weinberg 1977:38).

With the passing of the Emancipation Proclamation Act in 1863, which declared freedom for all enslaved people in Confederate-held territory, the broader and steady contact with White American English speakers drew African American English closer and closer to Standard American English, despite the many obstacles presented especially by southern states. The transition was so rapid that by the early 1900s all varieties could be understood, except for those spoken in very isolated communities (Weinberg 1977:39).

Today, African American English continues as a viable means of communication due to racial and class-based segregation, and because it is valued by its speakers as a sign of identity. Some middle-class African Americans can code switch from Standard American English to African American English when they choose to identify with the lower classes or to express intimacy, solidarity, and a friendly humor with other middle-class African Americans. It is often questioned, however, whether or not middle-class African Americans are actually proficient in this variety of English (for example, Weinstein 1983:105).

African American English, nonetheless, continues to be seen as presenting a problem in education and political participation, because working-class and lower-class African Americans cannot code switch to the English variety used in schools, government, commerce, and the media. Since many non-speakers of the variety have assumed that African American English speakers are "stupid" or "lazy," middle-class White and African American teachers and employers frequently penalize them (Weinstein 1983:105).

Thus, the debate continues over the role of African American English in schools. African American nationalists have cited the usefulness of the language, insisting that it be used as a medium of instruction and literature. Others, including Whites and some African Americans, have argued that legitimizing African American English in schools would close doors to upward mobility, because students would be less inclined to study Standard American English (Weinstein 1983:105).

In Ann Arbor, Michigan, for example, the debate went into the courtroom, because some parents of African American children insisted that the school board was breaking the law by not helping their children remove the linguistic barrier to education. These parents claimed denial of "equal educational opportunity," which is against the law. The judge, relying extensively on the testimonies of linguists, ruled in favor of the parents and ordered the school board to develop a program to help its teachers recognize the home language of the students and to use that knowledge in their attempts to teach reading skills in Standard American English. The school board quickly developed a course for teachers to enable them to understand the structure and importance of African American English and orient them to techniques that would help students learn how to code switch to Standard American English when appropriate (Weinstein 1983:105–106).

In New York City in the 1970s, teachers working with a group of young African American high school dropouts tried to recognize their distinct speech patterns and mold them into Standard American English. Dozens of public schools in Dallas, Los Angeles, and San Diego also have experimented with the idea over the last few decades. For years, some schools in different parts of the country have subtly been using similar strategies to help African American students learn how to read and write. These schools have heeded the advice of linguists that instead of trying to stamp it out, working with students' language variety for a while in class could be a sound educational approach (*Washington Post*, January 6, 1997:A1).

At their annual convention in 1997, leaders from the nation's urban schools spotlighted a series of programs that appeared to be helping African American students, particularly those from lower classes, make academic strides. One of them was the limited Ebonics program being offered in some of Oakland's most troubled public schools. The program, in which 3,000 of Oakland's African American students participate, was designed to teach Standard American English by first recognizing, and in part using, the distinct language habits they have learned in their communities. The focus of the program, which spends $200,000 a year in state and federal funds designated for poor children, is to train teachers and develop classroom materials that help students make the transition to Standard American English in ways that are not demeaning. In the years since Oakland initiated the program, it hardly received any local, much less national, attention. All that changed when the Oakland school board unanimously approved a resolution calling for a system-wide Ebonics program. After the vote, some Oakland school officials also suggested that the Ebonics resolution be used to seek federal and state funds for bilingual education. But U.S. secretary of education Richard W. Riley swiftly ruled that out (*Washington Post*, January 6, 1997:A10).

On January 3, 1997, the 6,000 member Linguistics Society of America (LSA), meeting in Chicago at its annual convention, stepped into the Oakland Ebonics debate by adopting a resolution that supported the school board's plans. Using African American English as a bridge to Standard American English might be effective in classrooms, the LSA members said (*Washington Post*, January 6, 1997:A1).

CHAPTER 5

THE SOCIAL CONSTRUCTION OF EBONICS: A FASOLDIAN PERSPECTIVE

As Ralph Fasold (2003), my former professor of linguistics and long-time scholar of African American English, recounts in his 2003 North West Centre of Linguistics Annual Lecture, it is common for linguistics textbooks to maintain that the concepts of "a language" and "a dialect" are not exclusively linguistic notions, but also involve political and social factors. Put differently, the distinction between what should be called a language or a dialect cannot be made on linguistic criteria alone, particularly on the basis of the common-sense criterion "mutual intelligibility." For example, a linguistics textbook written by Fromkin, Rodman, and Hyams (2002) that is widely used in the United States confesses that "Because neither mutual intelligibility nor the existence of political boundaries is decisive, it is not surprising that a clear-cut distinction between language and dialects has evaded linguistics scholars" (2002:446). In a similar vein, Peter Trudgill's popular textbook, Sociolinguistics: An Introduction to Language and Society, admits that "The criterion of 'mutual intelligibility', and other purely linguistic criteria, are, therefore, of less importance in the use of the terms language and dialect that are political and social and cultural factors ..." (1995:4). Nevertheless, regardless of how evasive or of less importance linguistic criteria are, most of the linguistics literature seems to suggest that linguistic criteria are crucial. Stated in another way, ultimately, the decision about what constitutes a language and what makes a dialect cannot be determined without linguistic expertise.

The crucial issue is whether or not one thinks it is possible that languages can be natural objects discoverable by employing methods of the natural sciences. If one thinks that there is no such possibility because *everything* is ultimately a social construct, then she or he will think that the point is too self-evident to be debated. Fasold's contention is that, while it is conceivable that languages might be scientifically discoverable natural objects, in fact they are not. Ulrich

Ammon (1989:31ff.) explicitly rejects this conclusion. Ammon argues that a political scientist would not accept a political system as a democracy just because its population calls it that, nor would a biologist consider an eel a snake because people consider it one. The difference is that political scientists can establish criteria to distinguish democracies from other kinds of political systems, and biologists can describe how to define snakes while excluding eels. Linguists, not for lack of effort, have been unable to determine criteria by which languages can be distinguished from dialects or other kinds of linguistic systems.

AUSBAU AND *ABSTAND* LANGUAGES

The problem of sociopolitical versus linguistic influences on assigning language or dialect status has been taken up by Heinz Kloss. He distinguishes between what he termed *ausbau* and *abstand* languages. An abstand language, a "language by distance," according to Kloss, is one that is so different from other related grammars that "a linguist would have to call it a language even if not a single word has ever been written in it" (1967:29). He is convinced that abstand language is "predominantly" a linguistic concept and "assume[s] that linguists are in a position to apply final, reliable and uniform criteria" on establishing status as languages for abstand languages (1967:30). Fasold argues that no such criteria exist or are likely to be discovered. In practice, then, according to Fasold, Kloss's notion is taken to mean that an abstand language is so distinct in linguistic properties from any language with which it might be associated that it would be obvious to any linguist that there exists a language and not a dialect.

Kloss's concept of "ausbau language," a "language by expansion," on the other hand, is fundamentally sociopolitical: i.e., ausbau languages have been deliberately reshaped to allow a wide range of literary expression. Fasold's own view is that elaboration for purposes of literary expression and the like is a rigid criterion. For Fasold, a language is a language if it has been socially constructed. If an existing social group believes and acts as if a linguistic system is a language, then it is a language.

Trudgill discusses the fate of the status of languages, depending, as he views it, on a combination of their abstand-ausbau properties and their socio-political circumstances. Trudgill emphasizes the fact that abstand is a relative concept and one can speak of degrees of abstand. The languages he refers to as *absolute* abstand languages—those, like Basque, that have no related languages anywhere—are, he believes, guaranteed status as separate languages regardless of the social setting. Of Basque, for example, Trudgill argues that "There is no possibility of claiming that it might be a dialect of some other language" (1992:168).

According to Fasold, other linguistic systems are part of dialect continua such as the West Germanic, West Romance, and North and South Slavic continua in Europe or, one might add, any number of similar continua elsewhere, like the Nguni and Sotho languages of South Africa, the Mayan languages of Mexico and Guatemala, and continua of Aryan languages in India. Whether these systems are considered languages or dialects, for Fasold, depends on social construction, with or without ausbau. Since this is the case, Fasold argues that status as a "language" can be created and dismantled over time.

For Fasold, returning to the question of whether or not languages are natural objects to be discovered by science, it seems clear to him that if the answer is yes, then the notion "ausbau language" is the oxymoron. He reasons that if there is such an object as a language, independent of its social construction, then one can no more make a dialect a language than an eel can be made into a snake by giving it a suit made of scales and letting it wiggle on the ground. He adds that if there is no such natural object, but language always and in every case must be socially constructed, then "abstand language" takes on the relatively trivial meaning—language so different from other surrounding linguistic systems that people are unlikely to construct it as a part of another language. Abstand then, he concludes, becomes ultimately a study of people's perceptions of difference.

SOCIAL CONSTRUCTION OF EBONICS AS A KIND OF ENGLISH

As noted earlier, *Ebonics* in the United States is most commonly constructed as a simplified, corrupted and broken approximation of Standard American English. This construction is virtually undisputed by most Americans, even by many African Americans. The United States has struggled with racism for more than two centuries, while at the same time adhering to an assimilationist ideology. The idea of assimilation applies to immigrants, who are expected to enter the "melting pot" and become thoroughly Americanized by, among other things, learning fluent American English and ceasing to use their heritage languages. It also applies to the native first Americans, who are indigenous to the North American continent, and to the descendants of enslaved Africans.

Similarly, the early days of the civil rights movement by and for African Americans emphasized "integration": i.e., the dismantling of laws that kept African Americans and European Americans from being educated in the same schools, eating in the same restaurants, or even using the same toilet facilities. The later emphasis on a distinct African American identity muted the integration ideal. The assimilationist perspective played a role in an early construction of American Ebonics as simply southern American English as spoken by the uneducated and disadvantaged. On this perspective, there was no substantial difference between the English of African Americans and that of European American disadvantaged southerners. Give African American speakers the same opportunities as most European Americans, and they would speak the standard dialect of their region. And, indeed, poor southern European Americans also spoke "Black English." It was all purely a matter of the combination of region and social inequality, nothing that could not be changed by integration.

As I pointed out earlier, during late 1996 and 1997, an action by the school board in Oakland, California, focused the light on Ebonics. The attacks on the language were often quite ridiculous. In opinion pieces around the nation, Ebonics was commonly assailed with such acrimonies like "a linguistic nightmare that refuses to die a natural death," "mumbo jumbo," "mutant English," "broken English," "fractured English," "ghettoese," and "the Ebonic plague." These monikers were often combined with the opinion that Ebonics is "bad" English that could be spoken by anyone, or with the facetious reference to other kinds of -onics, like "Ivoronics," which was supposed to be broken English as spoken by European Americans.

Since the middle of the last century, most mainstream American linguists, among others, have adopted the "salad bowl" or mosaic, rather than the "melting pot" (or integrationist), ideology of the desirable ethnic social organization for the United States. Each ethnic group could retain distinctions, including linguistic ones, and each of these groups contributed an ingredient or a tile to the total salad or mosaic of American social life. But it is ultimately a single pattern. Consequently, the motivation existed to construct Ebonics as a distinct and beautiful dialect of *English*. Just like the salad bowl or social mosaic, there existed a linguistic bowl or mosaic, with each ethnic dialect contributing its ingredient or tile to the whole American linguistic salad or mosaic.

Most frustrating for linguists was the futility of their efforts to construct AAE as a structured linguistic system, and thereby to break the subtle and destructive iconization of its speakers. A large part of this futility seems to stem from sharp differences between the everyday use of the terms "dialect" and "standard" and the linguists' use of the same terms. When AAE is defended as a systematic and well-ordered dialect, it is inevitably contrasted with "standard" English. But the term "standard" is of two types: minimum standards and arbitrary standards. Minimum standards are specifications that must be met or exceeded for acceptability. Safety standards for automobiles are an example. If an automobile lacks the right features and properties of structural integrity, it may fail the standards, and the manufacturer may not be able to sell it. In essence, minimum standards are imperative for an item to be considered "good enough." When minimum standards are lacking, the item has failed and should not be put into use.

Arbitrary standards are of a different sort. An example provided by Fasold is that the United States uses Fahrenheit degrees in measuring temperatures, including ambient air temperatures in weather reports. Most of the world measures temperatures in degrees Celsius. Fahrenheit degrees are harder to use and interpret and are based on less sensible criteria than Celsius degrees, and that the Fahrenheit system is, hence, inferior. However that may be, Fahrenheit degrees serve an important function as an agreed-upon arbitrary standard for people in the United States to understand and use. It is less important that the best system of temperature measurement is employed than it is that all Americans agree on the same—arbitrary—standard.

When linguists employ the term "standard language," they invariably and implicitly mean an arbitrary standard. There are advantages to have an agreement on certain arbitrary standards for some language uses. In American English, there is a general tacit agreement on what these standards are. The standard language may not be the best possible constellation of linguistic features available; in fact, Fasold has demonstrated elsewhere that in some ways (for example, in making distinctions among types and times of actions and states), standard English is demonstrably inferior to Ebonics. But just as there is general agreement in favor of the Fahrenheit standard, even if the Celsius standard is probably better, the arbitrary, agreed-upon standards for

American English are unlikely to be abandoned any time soon. It is general social acceptance that gives a workable arbitrary standard, not the inherent superiority of the item it specifies.

Fasold observes that in general conversation about language standards, however, the assumption made by the vast majority of people (who have not studied the nature of language in depth), is that the term "standard English" refers to *minimum* standards. If there is any variation from what is understood to the language standards, it is not seen as adherence to an alternative set of standards, but as a failure to achieve acceptable quality. Just like the house that fails to meet the building code standards, or an automobile that does not meet safety standards, nonstandard language is considered unfit to be used. The users of these dialects must, based on this view, be brought up to the minimum standard, for their own good as well as for the good of the society in general. In such a context, it seems like an oxymoron to speak of Ebonics or any variety other than standard English as "rule-governed." If a language fails to meet minimum standards, it has *eo ipso* failed to be governed by the only rules that count. It is impossible to hold the minimum standards view of standard English and still believe that nonstandard varieties are rule-governed. A variety may either be rule-governed or it may be nonstandard. It cannot, for most people, be both. When linguists assert that nonstandard varieties are rule-governed, although nonstandard, the perceived contradiction prevents us from making sense, or from being taken seriously.

At the height of the Oakland school board Ebonics debate, I was interviewed on German International Radio on January 15, 1997. Their offices are located at 3132 M Street, NW in the heart of Georgetown in Washington, D.C. During the interview with the two hosts, a male and a female, it was obvious they considered Ebonics as not meeting the standards to which everyone in America rises up; they rather Ebonics an instance of being lazy and going the other way.

Another view of the same problem involves the term "dialect." For linguists, dialects are speech varieties that make up a language, somewhat the way the slices make up the pie. One of these "slices" often achieves the status as a standard. But for the linguist, of course, this is an arbitrary standard. Given a different social history, one of the other dialects might have become the standard just as well.

For ordinary people, though, the term "dialect" and its relationship to the notion "language" is totally different. A "dialect" is either a speech system that is used by people who are considered primitive and that do not quite make it as a language (e.g., "the dialects of the indigenous people of the Amazon jungle"—note that they have "jungles" while we in the United States have "forests"—or it is a perhaps quaint but surely faulty way of speaking a "language." In that sense, it is comparable to slips of the tongue, slang-laced conversation, excessive use of profanity, and other perceived abuses of language. The linguist's view, as to be expected, is quite different.

Fasold asks us to imagine what happens when a linguist says that AAE is a dialect that is orderly and rule-governed and worthy of respect. The term "dialect" fits into the folk taxonomy for the audience, while the linguist is working with the linguistic taxonomy. The linguist thinks he has made a simple-to-understand statement that should be accepted on his authority as an expert on language. The statement is that the dialect AAE is one of a number of equally orderly dialects of English, including the standard one. The layperson, though, hears the word "dialect" and interprets it in terms of personal taxonomy. Since dialects are presupposed to be corruptions of language, the claim that AAE is orderly and rule-governed cannot make sense, unless it means that this particular way of corrupting the language has certain characteristics that can be described systematically. They may even agree that speakers of the dialect are worthy of respect. After all, one would not judge someone too harshly for the occasional slip of the tongue, so a person should not be too hard on someone who speaks a dialect once in a while. But the linguist's analysis will make no dent in the ordinary person's conviction that anyone who is able to speak only a dialect is in serious trouble. Such speakers have an immediate need to replace the dialect with the real language, perhaps being allowed to slip back into that particular kind of sloppiness in a few relaxed and casual settings, once the language is mastered. But the ordinary individual will never hear that the linguist is actually saying that the dialect AAE is on a par with the standardized dialect and, given different historical developments, might even have *been* the standard.

An exchange between the hosts and me during the same radio talk show mentioned earlier demonstrates that they implicitly held folk taxonomy and that I became caught in the no-man's-land between the linguistic and folk taxonomic understandings of the term "dialect." My only salvation was my making an analogy to the Plattdeutsches spoken in Switzerland and parts of Germany.

As Fasold points out, given the yawning chasm between linguistic and folk ideas of "standard" and "dialect," for linguists to convince the general public about our construction of AAE while using terms like "standard English" and "African American English dialect" starts us off immediately with a double handicap. Somehow, Fasold suggests, linguists have to dislodge the idea of minimum standards as applied to language and replace it with the alien concept of arbitrary standards. At the same time, linguists have to redefine "dialect" from a kind of corruption of the real language to a notion of dialect as a legitimate component of language relevant at a particular level of analysis. This done, linguists have to persuade listeners that, by the way, AAE is one of these co-dialects of English, which may deviate from the arbitrary standards imposed on English while conforming to standards of its own. Fasold concedes that the likelihood of accomplishing all this is quite small, despite the fact that AAE does have all the grammatical intricacies and capacity to make subtle grammatical distinctions that all language systems do. In some respects, it is able to make distinctions far more subtle than what is possible in standard English.

So far, as Fasold again concedes, this is the easier part of the argument—demonstrating that linguistic systems that are very close together may or may not achieve status as a separate language, depending entirely on ideological considerations. He asks whether United States Ebonics is the dialect of both disadvantaged African American and disadvantaged European American southerners, a sloppy degradation of English, or an elegantly ordered dialect of

American English. He responds by stating that the answer will hinge upon the responder's view of social order in the United States.

ABSTAND DIALECTS

For Fasold, this second part of the argument is more difficult, as the question is whether or not it would be possible to construct linguistic systems with substantial abstand as dialects of the *same* language. The case most often cited for this is Chinese, where many language systems that are so different from one another as to make them virtually mutually unintelligible are constructed as dialects of the Chinese language. In this case, though, the "dialects" are clearly related to each other, historically and in general structure. Presumably, the Chinese dialects fall short of what Trudgill calls "absolute Abstand," on the basis of which two languages can never be considered co-dialects, no matter what ideology might be served by doing so. A crucial problem with the notion "absolute abstand," of course, is the criteria by which it can be recognized—criteria which have never been proposed. But to explore this issue more closely, it makes sense to consider whether any language systems with abstand so great that it might be taken as absolute have ever been constructed as dialects of the same language. Fasold thinks that the answer is perhaps so.

EBONICS AS A LANGUAGE OF ABSTAND DIALECTS

As Fasold observes, a striking case in which language systems with substantial abstand may have been constructed as a single language involves another construction of Ebonics. The social construction of Ebonics is very much different from the construction of African American English or United States Ebonics. Ebonics is a language, or perhaps a family of languages, that unifies the people in the African diaspora, and is separate from the European languages with which it (or they) share most of the vocabulary and with which they may be mutually intelligible. This concept of Ebonics has been developed by scholars in the African-centric tradition. It is motivated by what they perceive as an attempt by European thinking to attribute most aspects of the history and culture of people of African descent outside of Africa to Western sources, thereby denying the agency of African people in these matters, and obscuring the unity of the people of the African diaspora over against the people of European origin among whom they live. The response is to propose that the language system spoken by people of African descent in the diaspora comprises a common language of African origin that is not to be mistaken for a variety of some European language, such as English or French.

To comprehend this argument more clearly, Fasold suggests that one needs to look more closely at what might count as abstand. Some languages can have considerable lexical and phonological similarity with one language, while displaying syntactic similarity to another. The case of Moldovian calqued on Russian is an example.

It is the assumption that language relationships are determined on the basis of syntactic and not on the basis of lexicon that African-centric scholars have argued for the unity of Ebonics and its distinction from English or any other European language. The position is explicitly articulated by Smith as follows:

> The fact is when one analyzes the grammars of the so-called "black English" dialect and the English spoken by the Europeans and Euro-Americans, the grammars are not the same. While there has been extensive borrowing or adoption of English and other European words, the grammar of the descendants of Niger-Congo African slaves follows the grammar rules of the Niger-Congo African languages...In other words, based on a criterion of continuity in the rules of grammar, there is no empirical evidence that "Black English" ever existed (1996:52).

Smith is arguing that Ebonics is a separate language from English, despite the frequency of words from the lexicon of English and other European languages on the same grounds that one might argue that some Moldovian constructions are really Russian—since the underlying grammatical structure, not vocabulary, is what counts for computing abstand.

Not only do African-centric linguists construct Ebonics as distinct from English, they also intend Ebonics to include other linguistic systems spoken by descendants of Africans. Blackshire-Belay (1996) is explicit on this point. She lists the following language systems as part and parcel of the Ebonics continuum:

IN NORTH AMERICA

Termed *Louisiana French Creole*. Used in parts of eastern Louisiana, but diminishing in numbers of speakers.

Termed *Black English* or *African American English*. English-based varieties spoken throughout the United States in African American communities, both rural and urban, south and north, male and female, and spoken among all socioeconomic groups.

IN SOUTH AMERICA

Termed *Brazilian Creole Portuguese*. Used by Brazilians of African ancestry in rural areas. This variety is spoken *in* Sao Paulo.

Termed *Língua Geral*. A Tupi-Guarrani-based variety used in Brazil. Now losing ground to Portuguese.

IN THE CARIBBEAN

Termed *Caribbean Creole English*. About 30 English-based varieties are found throughout the islands of the Caribbean, some represented by several varieties. The largest is the Ebonics spoken in Jamaica, with more than two million speakers.

Termed *Virgin Island Dutch Creole*. Widely used in the 19th Century, but now nearly extinct.

Blackshire-Belay includes English-, Dutch-, Portuguese-, French- and even Tupi-Guarani— lexified creoles along with Ebonics as spoken in the United States within the Ebonics continuum. She asserts:

> The most fascinating characteristic about these so-called pidgins and Creoles is that despite the fact they display many obvious differences in sounds, grammar, and vocabulary, they have a remarkable amount in common. Ebonics contains structural remnants of certain African languages, although the vocabulary is overwhelmingly English, French, or Spanish. My position is that Ebonics is rooted in the African experience, on the basis of the linguistic evidence reflected in the system and comparable to the system within many of the African languages of the Niger-Congo family, that is Twi, Igbo, Ewe, Efik (1996:20).

Indeed, what Blackshire-Belay speaks of is a family tree of Ebonics. Similarly, Africologist Robert Twiggs (1973) in some places speaks of a Pan-African language in the western hemisphere as a language; in other places, he speaks of it as a language *system*. Following through on the position taken by Smith and apparently endorsed, at least in part, by Blackshire-Belay, Fasold suggests that there would be no reason not to take all the points on Blackshire-Belay's continuum as dialects of the same language. That is, if what counts is syntactic structure and not vocabulary, then a language lexified by French is the same language as a language lexified by English, as long as both are based on the same grammar.

Even more important is the fact that African-centric scholars do not rest their case only on the supposed structural substrate from African languages, but also on thought patterns, gestures, and other criteria beyond nuts-and-bolts linguistics. As Smith puts it,

> In the sense that Ebonics includes both the verbal and paralinguistic communications of African Amercan people, this means that Ebonics represents an underlying psychological thought process. Hence, the non-verbal sounds, cues, gestures, and so on that are systematically used in the process of communication by African American people are encompassed by the term as well (1996:54).

And Blackshire-Belay adds: "Nonverbal communication patterns in African culture, for example, rhetorical style, body movement, expressions, gestures, are included in the process" (1996:20 fn. 2).

Ebonics, then, can only be partially constructed by means of the Eurocentric standard practices of linguistics. And since Eurocentric linguistics has no privileged position in this regard, there is no reason why the construction of a language from such apparently absolute abstand varieties as United States Ebonics and French Haitian Creole should not succeed.

The ideology that is being promoted by the construction of Ebonics as a language, or at least as a continuum of related languages, is not hard to discern. Focusing on the undeniable and continuing effects of slavery and present-day racism perpetrated by people of European origin, African-centric scholars seek grounds on which all those of African origin who have had and are having this experience can be unified, and at the same time separated from European-origin society. They are dismayed that so much of the lives and cultures of people who trace their origins to Africa is explained by Eurocentric scholarship as having ultimately European origins, even if perhaps shaped by their unique experiences as Africans. It then seems reasonable to look for origins for present-day cultural institutions in the African diaspora in Africa, at a time when African people have the luxury of agency to develop their traditions without the interference of European oppressors. Ebonics the language, then, becomes iconic to all that unifies people of African origin as against Europe-based societies in which they live. In fact, these considerations are not so different from many of the cases of the construction of ausbau languages described in Kloss (1967) and Trudgill (1992), among others.

In essence, African-centric scholars have satisfactorily constructed Ebonics as a language of abstand dialects. In fact, this construction of Ebonics briefly became part of official policy in one school district in one city in the United States, during the Oakland, California, Ebonics debate of 1996 and 1997 discussed earlier.

EBONICS NEED NOT BE ENGLISH

In his issue paper entitled "Ebonics Need Not Be English" (1999), Fasold proffers an even more radical view on Ebonics, that the language need not be English, by raising and addressing the following questions: (a) What does it take to make a language? (b) Is Ebonics bad English? (c) Is Ebonics a language or a dialect? (d) Why consider Ebonics a separate language? But before addressing these questions, Fasold first points out that the term *Ebonics* is not an appropriate name for a linguistic entity. However, he adds, the coinage is actually very close to a natural way of naming languages. He notes that there are languages that end in *-ic*, like Arabic and Amharic, as well as language family names of that form, like Slavic and Germanic. Thus, Ebonics, in such a naming system, is a clear way to specify *Black Language*. The following is a synopsis of his arguments in sequential order.

WHAT DOES IT TAKE TO MAKE A LANGUAGE?

As Fasold points out, linguists generally agree that the notion of a language is largely, or entirely, sociopolitical. The requirement for the makeup of a language encompasses more than just a set of structural linguistic properties or lack of intelligibility with related linguistic systems; it also includes the conviction that the linguistic system in question is a symbol of nationalist or ethnic identity. Examples exist around the world of the two logical possibilities of cases in which mutually unintelligible linguistic varieties belong to the same language and other cases where mutually intelligible varieties are separate languages. For example, the Chinese dialects are distinct from one another, at least as much as the Romance languages; yet, they remain dialects of the Chinese language. An example of the other type is the constellation of languages that includes Dutch, Flemish, and Afrikaans. Each of these languages is easily understood by speakers of the others; yet, for most Afrikaaners, Afrikaans is certainly neither Dutch nor Flemish, but a new language that grew from the South African soil. Similarly, many Belgian Flemings do not even entertain the idea to accept Flemish as a dialect of Dutch. These examples show that linguistically similar varieties can be languages if they are identified with different countries. The Nguni language family of South Africa demonstrates that linguistically similar varieties can be separate languages even if they are spoken within the same country. The four Nguni languages—Ndebele, Swati, Xhosa, and Zulu—are readily understood by speakers of the others. Nevertheless, proposals to unify the languages of this group into a single standard language have encountered stiff resistance, mainly because of the general belief that the languages to be unified are each languages in their own right.

Thus, for Fasold, no linguistic or geographical reason exists for Ebonics not to achieve status as a language distinct from English. The two objections to the proposition he envisions are the following: (1) that Ebonics is not a language, but rather English corrupted by bad grammar and excessive slang; and (2) that Ebonics and English are too similar to each other to be different languages.

IS EBONICS BAD ENGLISH?

As Fasold notes, the idea that Ebonics is "bad" English is obviously false to linguists who have studied it in detail (e.g., Mufwene et al. 1998, Wolfram and Schilling-Estes 1998). However, outside the realm of academic linguistics, the notion that Ebonics is "bad" is generally held to be incontrovertibly true. Thus, it is necessary to show that this idea is untenable. It is clear on examination that Ebonics, far from being "bad" English, is actually superior to English in one of its subsystems: the verbal tense aspect system. In addition to the verb structure that English also has, Ebonics provides its speakers with rich resources for making distinctions among kinds and times of actions and states that can be made in English only awkwardly through the use of a longer and more awkward expression. For example, Ebonics possesses several aspect markers; one is the habitual, exemplified as follows:

(a) He be lookin/he do be lookin.
He is sometimes/usually/always looking.

(b) He don't be lookin.
He is not sometimes/usually/always looking.

The preceding forms are often used as illustrative that Ebonics is simply corrupt English. The habitual is invariably used ungrammatically in such illustrations, where it is taken as a corruption of "He is looking." Of course, the habitual progressive in Ebonics contrasts with the present progressive, which would be "He lookin" or, under emphasis, "He *is* lookin." It also contrasts with the simple present. It would be perfectly reasonable, for example, for an Ebonics speaker to say "She not singin right now, but she be singin mostly every day, and she sing good." This would mean that the person referred to is not in the process of singing at the moment, but that one would find her in the process of singing almost daily, and that she characteristically sings well.

According to Fasold, such verb forms are frequently cited as evidence of slovenly English. Under analysis, however, they are shown to fit into an impressive verbal system that functions more efficiently than the English system does. Once this becomes clear, it is amazing to see Ebonics presented as superior to English. The three-way distinction in Ebonics among the present, the present progressive, and the habitual progressive contrasts with a more limited two-way distinction between the present and present progressive in English.

IS EBONICS A LANGUAGE OR A DIALECT?

For Fasold, while the second objection that Ebonics and English are too similar to be different languages is overtly or tacitly considered valid even by linguists, the argument is also faulty. To demonstrate, he looks at another speech system that is similar to English: Scots. One of the three languages of Scotland, Scots is a Germanic language that was once the language of the court and that has largely been displaced by English. Due to its relatedness to English, Scots is now considered by many in Scotland to be a corrupted dialect of English, a similar attitude to the one directed toward Ebonics in the United States. The differences between Scots and English seem comparable to those between Ebonics and English, as the following example from a World Wide Web site maintained by Clive P. L. Young illustrates (www.umist.ac.uk/UMIST_CAL/Scots/haunbuik.htm):

> Scots: *The wirdleet kivvets aboot 700 o the maist cowmon wirds in onie leid (A wisna luikin fur jist kenspeckle Scots wirds). The spellins come frae the School Scots Dictionary. A warnin thou, the file is muckle an maun tak a wee tae doonload.*
> English Translation: *The word list covers about 700 of the most common words in any language (I wasn't just looking for well-known Scots words). The spellings are*

from the School Scots Dictionary. A warning, though, the file is large and may take a while to download.

To the uninitiated, the Scots version for the most part looks like English badly spelled. There are a few vocabulary differences, like "kenspeckle," "leid," and "muckle," but most of the excerpt contains words that are close cognates of English words. Historically, and in the view of present-day activists, however, Scots is not a degenerate form of English, but a language distinct from English. Merlin Press, a small publishing house that puts out instructional materials for teaching Scots, has posted the following questions and answers on its Web site (www. sol.co.uk/m/merlinpress):

Q. In what form does Scots exist in the present day?

A. It exists in a multiplicity of dialect forms but without a Standard Scots to correspond to Standard English. There is nothing linguistically wrong with the forms of Scots we have, but for political and social reasons our children have been discouraged from using them for nearly three hundred years, on the grounds that they are incorrect, inferior or corrupt forms of English.

Q. Isn't Scots just a form of slang?

A. Absolutely not. When teaching Scots, one of your first tasks will be to show children the difference between Scots and slang.

Q. What is the best way to teach Scots in the classroom?

A. The best way is to start with what you have: The children themselves hear Scots every day, and many of them actually speak it without realising it. Start by recognizing this and allowing its use in the classroom.

To those who followed the Ebonics debate, the preceding discourse has an almost eerie familiarity. Scots has to be defended from charges that it is an incorrect form of English and just slang. Children grow up speaking Scots but are discouraged from using it. The suggestion in answer to the question, "What is the best way to teach Scots in the Classroom?", is almost identical to the proposal by the Oakland School Board that provoked the furor in late 1996 and early 1997, except that the Oakland School Board proposed the use of Ebonics in the classroom as a bridge to English.

It is evident that Scots as a linguistic variety is seen by some as a corrupted dialect of English but also having status as a language. As a language, Scots has important advantages over Ebonics. It has its own recognized grammar and dictionary. It is taught as a subject at several of Scotland's oldest universities. While not widely taught at the primary and secondary school levels, it is not considered outrageous to teach Scots in these schools, and there are published materials for use in teaching it.

On the other hand, as Fasold also points out, Ebonics has one great advantage over Scots. It appears that without successful efforts to maintain and revive it, Scots is in danger of dying out completely in a few generations. Ebonics, in spite of an almost universal opinion against it and a total lack of support for it in the American educational system, is one of the most robustly maintained minority languages in existence. There is no hint that it is in any danger of dying out in the foreseeable future.

WHY CONSIDER EBONICS A SEPARATE LANGUAGE?

Fasold argues that there are several advantages to considering Ebonics a language separate from English rather than as an orderly and systematic dialect of English. The major advantage is that when one speaks of Ebonics as a language rather than as a dialect, it reforms the discourse in a way that makes it easier to address the common misconceptions about Ebonics that have kept the debate at such an uninformed level. To begin with, when Ebonics is defended as a systematic and well-ordered dialect, it is inevitably contrasted with *standard* English. As pointed out earlier, the concept *standard* has two meanings: (1) minimum standards—i.e., specifications that must be met for acceptability; and (2) arbitrary standards—i.e., agreed-upon standards that everyone understands and uses. However, as also pointed out earlier, the assumption made by the vast majority of people who have studied the nature of language in depth is that the term *standard English* refers to minimum standards. The users of these dialects must, in this view, be brought up to the minimum standard, for their own good as well as for the good of the society as a whole.

Another problem also mentioned earlier involves the term *dialect*. For the linguist, dialects are speech varieties that make up a language. For the general public, though, a dialect is a perhaps quaint but very faulty way of speaking a language. In that sense, it is on a par with slips of the tongue, slang-laced conversation, excessive use of profanity, and other perceived abuses of language. The linguist's notion is quite to the contrary. For the linguist, there are several levels of analysis of a language, each just a different perspective of the same phenomenon. The language is the largest level, but it can be viewed in greater detail as the dialects of which it is composed, and these, in turn, can be more closely examined as the various styles of each dialect.

As mentioned earlier, when linguists refer to Ebonics as a dialect of English, they intend to make a simple-to-understand statement that the dialect Ebonics is one of a number of equally ordered dialects of English, including the standard one. It is not comparable to slurred speech or slips of the tongue, which lie at a much lower level of language analysis. The non-linguist, though, interprets the word *dialect* in this way. Since dialects are presumed by the non-linguist to be corruptions of language, the truism that Ebonics is orderly and rule-governed makes no sense. The linguist's appeal will make no dent in the non-linguist's conviction that anyone who is capable of speaking only a dialect has an immediate need of replacing the dialect with the "real language." This person will not even entertain the idea that the dialect Ebonics is on par with the standardized dialect and, given different historical developments, might even have been the standard.

As also noted earlier, Fasold argues that for linguists to attempt to convey what we have learned about Ebonics, using terms like *standard English* and *African American English Dialect* starts us off immediately with a double handicap. Therefore, he suggests that we dislodge the idea of minimum standards as applied to language and replace it with the concept of arbitrary standards. At the same time, he adds, we must redefine dialect, moving away from the notion of dialect as a corruption of the real language to a notion of dialect as a legitimate component of all languages. On the other hand, he adds, if Ebonics were a language and not a dialect, it would not be assumed to be a corruption of anything. Each language has its own standards. Consequently, the standards of some other language are simply irrelevant. The way we discuss these matters would then have to change. Fasold then asks us to imagine to following hypothetical discourse:

Q: Isn't Ebonics just bad English?

A: Linguist: certainly Ebonics is bad English, in the same sense that French is bad English. English is bad Ebonics, too.

Q: Why don't these so-called Ebonics speakers inflect the verb "to be"? Why do they say "He be eatin" when they mean "He is eating?"

A: Linguist: Unlike English which has only one form for "to be," Ebonics has two words for "to be." One of them is inflected and the other is not. The grammar of Ebonics makes a distinction not found in English. The difference is quite subtle and not easy for English speakers to master.

Fasold concludes with the following observation:

Simply speaking of Ebonic(s) as a language rather than a dialect will not immediately cause linguists' discoveries about Ebonic(s) to become universally accepted. There would be massive resistance to the idea that Ebonic(s) is a language. Even if by dint of charisma and eloquence linguists manage to convince some non-linguists that Ebonic(s) could be a language, the struggle would not be over. However, I would find the new struggle easier to deal with. I know that, at least in teaching my own students, I have been able to get across the linguistic perception of the nature of Ebonic(s) much more efficiently by framing its relation to English as one of language to language.

How poignant, indeed!

CHAPTER 6

✝

THE OAKLAND UNIFIED SCHOOL DISTRICT (OUSD) INITIATIVE

In the nation's public schools, the academic record of many poor African American students is dismal and getting worse. For instance, the Oakland Unified School District (OUSD) reports that 53 percent of its total enrollment of 51,706 is African American; 71 percent of the students enrolled in special education programs are African American; 64 percent of students held back are African American; 71 percent of African American males attend school on an irregular basis; 19 percent of the 12th grade African American students did not graduate the 1995–1996 school year; 80 percent of all suspended students are African American; and the 1.80 average grade point average (GPA) for African American students represents the lowest GPA in the District (OUSD 1996).

Frustrated educators searched for dramatic new ways to get at one root of the problem: language skills. OUSD contends that African American English is the primary language of many of its African American students, who may fall behind in school because the language they use at home and in their communities may be different from the Standard American English used in the classroom.

On December 18, 1996, the OUSD Board of Education approved a policy affirming Standard American English language development for all students. This policy mandates that effective instructional strategies, including Ebonics, must be utilized to ensure that every child has the opportunity to achieve English language proficiency. The board recognizes English language proficiency as the foundation for competency in all academic areas. The policy is based on the work of a broad-based task force convened in May of 1996 to review the district-wide achievement data and to make recommendations regarding effective practices that would enhance the opportunity for all students to successfully achieve the standards of the core curriculum (OUSD 1996).

One of the board's recommendations is the Standard English Proficiency (SEP) program, a State of California model program, which promotes English language development for African American students. The SEP training enables teachers and administrators to respect and acknowledge the history, culture, and language that the African American student brings to school. By recognizing Ebonics, OUSD officials said they hoped to improve the way African American students are taught to read and write Standard American English (OUSD 1996).

The Board adopted a policy on teaching English, not Ebonics. Unfortunately, because of misconceptions in the resulting press stories, the actions of the board have been publicly misunderstood. The misconceptions include the following: OUSD has decided to teach Ebonics in place of Standard American English; OUSD is trying to classify Ebonics-speaking students as bilingual; OUSD is trying to get federal and state funds; OUSD is trying to create a system of perverse incentives that reward failure and lower standards; OUSD is condoning the use of slang; Ebonics further segregates an already racially divided school district; and there is no statistical evidence to support this approach or that this approach will improve student achievement (OUSD 1996).

However, the fact is that OUSD is not replacing the teaching of Standard American English with any other language. The district is not teaching Ebonics. (This would be redundant, as the students in question already speak the language.) Rather, the district's objective is to build on the language skills African American students bring to the classroom without humiliating and degrading them and their diversity (OUSD 1996).

Compared with skin color, language offers far more opportunities to discriminate. People speak approximately 5,000 different languages around the world, about 3,000 of them in Africa alone. Countless dialects—or varieties of mother tongues—enrich the global linguistic spectrum further (Washington Post January 6, 1997:A10). For example, a good friend of mine recently informed me about a letter her friend showed her from an Egyptian friend who lives in Egypt. The first line of the letter was "What's up," a phrase originated and made popular by African Americans.

The attempts of OUSD to find a way to bridge the communication gap between educators and students are to be applauded, not chastised. In many parts of the country, African American teachers are almost nonexistent. Students matriculate all the way from kindergarten to the 12th grade and never have an African American teacher. For the most part, educators come from middle-class environments. Therefore, we have an abundance of situations where lower-income African American students are taught by middle-class White instructors. Thus, we have cultural and economic gaps where the teacher may assume his or her status to be superior and the student's status inferior. Certainly, in situations like these, the academic performance of the student is affected by the perceptions of the teacher.

The OUSD decision helps teachers bridge the language gap and develop greater understanding for the cultural diversity the African American student brings to the classroom. Teachers who want their students to foster creativity and independent thinking will be amazed at the richness Ebonics will bring to the classroom. For example, a friend of mine recently taught a fifth grade social studies class, where the students were studying the 50 states. She used the melodies of old "Negro Spirituals" and changed the lyrics to that of the names of the states in specific regions. Not only did the children enjoy the songs, but she heard them singing them on the playground and when they were going home. Since she had legitimized the use of her culture in the learning process, the students understood it was okay to do the same. Several of the African American male students developed Ebonics rap lyrics to add to the songs whose melodies she had borrowed from our ancestors. At the end-of-the-year school closing ceremony, she and her students sang the songs, rap and all, to the delight of parents, faculty, and other students. Those students will remember those songs and, consequently, the regions and the states, for years to come. Indeed, Ebonics can be a very powerful tool!

CHAPTER 7

LINGUISTIC CONNECTIONS BETWEEN THE AFRICAN, JAMAICAN AND NEGRO NATIONAL ANTHEMS

One out of every five Africans lives outside the African continent. The great majority of these Africans are in the western hemisphere. Some are now native speakers of Spanish, like the African Cubans. Some have grown up with the Portuguese tongue, like the African Brazilians. Still others are part of the French-speaking world, scattered from Haiti to Martinique. There are also a few Arabic speakers throughout the Middle East. But the largest single group outside the African continent comprises African Saxons: that is, African Americans, African Jamaicans, African Trinidadians, African Britons, and African Canadians (Mazrui 1977:68).

The slave trade was the most significant catalyst in dispersing Africans to other parts of the world. But it was not until late in the 19th century, and in the course of the 20th century, that pan-Africanism as a movement of African solidarity got underway (Mazrui 1977:68). This led to a significant number of investigations about linguistic, social, and cultural connections between Africa and its diaspora.

However, as stated earlier, the debate over the linguistic, social, and cultural connections between Africa and the diaspora has been controversial since Melville J. Herskovits's pioneering work was published in 1941. The debate was heightened when E. Franklin Frazier's work appeared in 1963. While Herskovits proposed that African linguistic, social, and cultural features have survived in North America and have been retained by a process of acculturation and adaptation, Frazier emphasized African linguistic, social, and cultural discontinuity and advocated a deculturalization hypothesis.

What all these works demonstrate is that, as also mentioned earlier, the almost total absence of visible African artifacts in African diaspora culture does not warrant the view that nothing African survived the tyranny of slavery. While the visible artifacts of religious sculpture gradually disappeared, subtler linguistic and communicative artifacts were sustained and embellished by the Africans' creativity. What this chapter does is survey some of these complex linguistic connections, which constitute continuity and relationship between Africa and its diaspora.

Toward this end, this chapter presents a textual analysis of three African diasporic anthems: the African National Anthem ("Nkosi Sikelel' iAfrika"), the Jamaican National Anthem ("Jamaica"), and the Negro National Anthem ("Lift Ev'ry Voice and Sing"). By analyzing the texts of these anthems using presuppositions,[1] within a linguistic framework,[2] it is suggested that previous studies that have examined national anthems and other textual political symbols,[3] in terms of their valuable functions in the lives of political systems, are quite limited for understanding their meanings. An examination of the texts of the three anthems clearly shows that national anthems, like other textual political symbols, convey not only surface contents, but a great deal of auxiliary contents as well. The major thesis in this chapter, then, is the following: Analyses of national anthems or other textual political symbols that fail to account for linguistic presuppositions risk ignoring relevant contents that may be central to the texts' meanings.

Consequently, this chapter is also about the possibility that significant functional explanations of textual political symbols can be evaluated using linguistic features. The essence of an approach of this nature is captured by Levinson (1983:40) when he suggests:

> Most recent linguistic explanations have tended to be internal to linguistic theory: that is to say, some linguistic feature is explained by reference to other linguistic features, or to aspects of the theory itself. But there is another possible kind of explanation, often more powerful, in which some linguistic feature is motivated by principles outside the scope of linguistic theory.

Available analyses of textual political symbols have been conducted by political analysts. But because these political analysts lack the necessary tools for delineating the linguistic structures inherent in these textual political symbols, their analyses have been limited to functional explanations.

By employing a presuppositional approach to analyze the texts of the three national anthems, the ideas underlying these political symbols can be illuminated. This is possible because in the study of linguistic texts, as in the study of physics, special instruments, formulas, and laboratories beyond the grasp of the uninitiated can be utilized. Someone trained in linguistics possesses analytical skills, tools, and concepts that permit insights into the nature of language in general. The linguist is in a better position than a political analyst to explain the formal linguistic structures that constitute cues about the writers' intentions for others interpreting their textual political symbols.

Thus, the major question in this chapter is the following: What salient linguistic presuppositions are embedded in the texts of the three national anthems, and how can they be explained? In exploring this question, the systematic application of well-known discovery procedures in linguistic pragmatics will help uncover propositions that will illuminate the texts for current readers.

In order to accomplish the preceding objectives, the rest of this chapter is divided into four interrelated major sections: (1) Synopsis of Previous Studies on Political Symbols, (2) Methodology, (3) Contexts of the Discourses of the Three National Anthems, and (4) Analysis. The originality of this chapter consists, therefore, in the clarity with which familiar but unconnected facts about the texts of the three national anthems are marshaled into a simpler, linguistically satisfying unity.

SYNOPSIS OF PREVIOUS STUDIES ON POLITICAL SYMBOLS

Previous studies on political symbols have examined such symbols in terms of their valuable functions in the lives of political systems. They are said to be important in promoting social integration, fostering legitimacy, inducing loyalty, gaining compliance, and providing citizens with security and hope (Edelman 1964, Jones 1964, Lasswell 1965, Merelman 1966, Cobb and Elder 1976 and 1983).

Because these studies have done very little empirical research on what political symbols mean to the public (more specifically, the American Constitution), Bass (1979) takes the first step toward examining the symbolic meaning of the American Constitution and its development. Using Q sort, correlation, and factor analysis statistical techniques, Bass finds that the Constitution is a vague, diffuse and distant symbol that is given specific meaning in terms of concrete primary figures and/or images.

While all of these studies are quite useful for understanding political symbols, they nevertheless tell us nothing about the auxiliary contents of these symbols, especially the textual ones. The relevant contents that may be central to the meanings of these symbols therefore need to be explored. The question that emerges here, then, is the following: How can this be done?

METHODOLOGY

As stated in the introductory section of this chapter, the method employed here to analyze the texts of the three national anthems is linguistic presuppositional analysis. This approach is based on the premise that there exist in every discourse some background assumptions against which the main import of utterances or statements can be assessed (Levinson 1983:173).

The rhetorical tactic of presupposition in political discourse is by now familiar to many linguists. A paradigm example is the opponent's query, "Has the president stopped siphoning the country's funds to his Swiss bank account?" Without explicitly making the assertion, the opponent implicates that the president has indeed been siphoning the country's funds to his Swiss bank account. Less contentious presuppositions can be suggested as well: that the president is a male, and that the president has a Swiss bank account. This example illustrates the fact that speakers or writers often express more than they assert. Their utterances or scripts convey not only their surface contents, but a great deal of auxiliary content as well.

In the data analysis section, the linguistic presuppositions extracted from the texts of the three national anthems are identified and analyzed. In the remainder of this section, the concept (presupposition) is defined and its scope clearly delimited. This is done by briefly examining the concept as it has developed in the philosophical and linguistic literature.[4]

LOGICAL PRESUPPOSITION

The phenomenon of linguistic presupposition can be traced back to the philosophical writings of Gottlob Frege (1892/1952). He raised many of the issues that later became central to the discussion of presupposition. According to Frege, "If anything is asserted there is always an obvious presupposition (Voraussetzung) that the simple or compound proper names used have a reference" (1952:69).

A later exchange between Bertrand Russell (1905, 1957) and Peter Strawson (1950, 1952) brought the notion of presupposition more fully into scholarly discourse. Russell, in his first essay on the subject (1905), argued that Frege's views were simply wrong. Struggling with the problem of how to account for the fact that sentences lacked proper referents, Russell came up with conclusions that were different from those of Frege.

Russell's analysis remained unchallenged until Strawson, in his 1950 essay, suggested a different approach. For Strawson, many of the puzzles in Russell's essay emerged from a failure to distinguish sentences from uses of sentences to make, for instance, statements that are true or false. Consider the following sentences.

1. The President of the United States is a tyrant.
2. The President of the United States is not a tyrant.
3. There is one and only one President of the United States.

In his analysis of definite descriptions, Russell suggested that propositions of the form (1) entail presuppositions of the form (3). Strawson did not agree with this suggestion. Instead, Strawson pointed out that (2), the negation of (1), does not affect the truth conditions of (3). If the relation between (1) and (3) were one of entailment, then, by modus ponens[5] (2) could not entail (3). One's linguistic intuitions tell him/her, however, that if either (1) or (2) is true, then (3) is also true. Strawson labeled the relation one of presupposition, which he formally designated as:

4. Sentence S_1 logically presupposes sentence S_2 iff the truth of S_2 is a precondition for She truth or falsity of S_1 (1952:175).

The practical approach for distinguishing presuppositions from entailments is the employment of the traditional constancy under negation rule. One sentence is said to presuppose another if and only if the sentence and its negation both require it to be true.

SEMANTIC PRESUPPOSITION AND IMPLICATIONS FOR LOGIC

Intrigued by Strawson's account of presupposition, formal linguists sought to build semantic theory upon the foundational relation of semantic entailment defined in (5), and had hoped to advance a more convincingly logical account of natural language by suggesting the relation of semantic presupposition defined in (6), as follows:

5. S_1 semantically entails S_2 (written S_1, $\Vdash S$), iff every situation that makes S_1 true makes S_2 true.
6. A sentence S_1 semantically presupposes a sentence S_2 iff $S_1 \Vdash S$ and $\sim S_1 \Vdash S_2$.

In order to incorporate the relation of semantic presupposition into a formal natural-language semantics, a logical framework that is different from the standard calculi is called for. This means that bivalence[6] and modus tollens[7] must be given up in order to meet the requirement for semantic presupposition. If a sentence S1 semantically presupposes a sentence S2, then, by definition (6), S1 entails S2 and ~S1 entails S2. Modus tollens must thus be given up. For without bivalency, in propositions of the form p6q, the falsity of the consequent could not falsify the condition. The consequent might instead result in the truth value "neither true nor false."

PRESUPPOSITIONAL DEFEASIBILITY

Presuppositional defeasibility refers to the fact that presuppositions are liable to evaporate in certain contexts, either immediate linguistic contexts, less immediate discourse contexts, or in cases where contrary assumptions are made. The defeasibility of presuppositions in particular discourse contexts, for example, can defeat any context-free semantic account as illustrated below:

7. Kwame Nkrumah was overthrown from the presidency before he could realize his dream of a united Africa.
8. Kwame Nkrumah realized his dream of a united Africa.
9. Kwame Nkrumah died before he could realize his dream of a united Africa.

The connectives 'before' and 'after' ordinarily trigger the presuppositions of their complements, as (7) presupposes (8). But in (9), the meaning of 'before' (temporal priority) plus background knowledge about death defeat the presupposition of (8). Individuals ordinarily do not realize their dreams after their deaths.

In this situation, temporal logic will not help. Presuppositions are defeasible within many constructions such as those in the following sentences.

10. If Robert Mugabe invites Charles Taylor to Zimbabwe, he will regret having a murderer as his guest.

11. If Robert Mugabe invites Thabo Mbeki to Zimbabwe, he will regret having a murderer as his guest.

12. Robert Mugabe will have a murderer as his guest.

The sentence (11) presupposes (12), but (10) does not. Since Charles Taylor is well known for his murderous campaigns in Liberia whose invitation Robert Mugabe will regret, the conditional clause in (10) defeats the presupposition of (12). The fact that Thabo Mbeki is not generally thought to be a murderer, 'murderer' in (11) must refer to someone else and the conditional clause does not defeat the presupposition.

Examples such as this would place presupposition outside the domain of context-free logical semantics, but within the scope of a context-sensitive linguistic semantics. The incorporation of propositions drawn from lexical entries, nonetheless, fails to account for all forms of presuppositional defeasibility. The contents of the discourse below, for example, can defeat a presupposition.

13. We need to find out which African leaders are on the payroll of the United States Central Intelligence Agency (CIA). John Stockwell would certainly know. I have discussed the issue with him. John Stockwell is not aware that Mobutu is on the payroll of the CIA. So John Stockwell can be trusted.

The sentence "John Stockwell is not aware that Mobutu is on the payroll of the CIA" would ordinarily presuppose that "Mobutu is on the payroll of the CIA." But the preceding discourse defeats this presupposition. It appears that any semantics of presupposition, then, calls for access to the discourse context in order to detect defeated presuppositions. As in the case of lexical access, the mechanisms needed to account for presuppositions gravitate away from semantics and toward pragmatics in this case as well.

Iterative presuppositional defeat causes more havoc. Consider this example.

14. It isn't Buthelezi who will become our next head of state.

15. Someone will become our next head of state.

Ordinarily, sentence (14) will presuppose sentence (15). Suppose, however, that each potential head of state in South Africa had asked the utterer of (14), "Will I be the next head of state?" to which the response is "No." By iterating over the set of potential heads of state and proposing that each, in turn, will not be the next head of state, the presupposition in (15) is defeated. Appeals to lexical knowledge will definitely fail to explain the defeat of the presupposition in this example. Reference to the deictic context[8] of the discourse is necessary in order to explain the defeat of the presupposition of (15).

THE PROJECTION PROBLEM

There exist two sides to the projection problem. The first is that presuppositions tend to survive in linguistic contexts where entailments cannot. More precisely, the presuppositions of component sentences are inherited by the whole complex sentence where the entailments of those components would not be. The second is that presuppositions tend to disappear in other contexts where one might expect them to survive, and where entailments would.

Beginning with the kind of context in which presuppositions survive where entailments do not, the examples that follow suggest that one may, but need not, take this as a defining characteristic of presuppositions.

16. The President appointed five Negro sellouts.
17. There is a President.
18. The President appointed three Negro sellouts.

If sentence (16) is negated, as in (19), the entailment (18) does not survive, but the presupposition (17) does; this being of course the initial observation from which presuppositional theories emerged.

19. The President did not appoint five Negro sellouts.

In a similar manner, presuppositions survive in other kinds of contexts in which entailments do not. An example is modal contexts: that is, those embedding under modal operators such as possible, may be, most probably, etc. Consequently, (20) continues to presuppose (17).

20. It is possible that the President appointed five Negro sellouts.

It is obvious, however, that (20) does not entail (18). One cannot logically infer from the mere possibility of a state of affairs that any part of it is actual.

Presuppositions tend to distinguish themselves by their ability to survive in different sets of contexts like compound sentences formed by connectives and, or, if … then and their equivalents. Consider the following examples.

21. The two chief's sons are hired again this term,
    which entails inter alia, (22) and presupposes (23) because of the iterative again.

22. A chief's son is hired this term.
23. The two chief's sons had been hired before.

If (21) is embedded in the antecedent of a conditional like in (24),

24. If the two chief's sons are hired again this term, Lansana Conte will get the support he desperately needs,

it is evident that (22) is not an entailment of (24), but the presupposition (23) survives.

Now turning to the second aspect of the projection problem, in which presuppositions of lower clauses sometimes fail to be inherited by the whole complex sentence, one would observe that presuppositions are sometimes defeasible because of intra-sentential context.

Presuppositions can be overtly denied in co-ordinate sentences such as these:

25. Chinua Achebe didn't manage to become President.
26. Chinua Achebe tried to become President.
27. Chinua Achebe didn't manage to become President; he didn't even run.

Here, (25) presupposes (26), but overt denial defeats it in (27).

In addition, to the overt denial of presuppositions, they can also be suspended in conditional clauses, as for example in the following:

28. Yoweri Museveni didn't lie to the Liberian people again about leaving office.
29. Yoweri Museveni previously lied to the Liberian people about leaving office.
30. Yoweri Museveni didn't lie to the Liberian people again about leaving office; if indeed he ever did.

In this example, (28) presupposes (29), but the condition in (30) defeats it.

In sum, the preceding discussion clearly suggests that semantic theories of presupposition are not viable. This is mainly because semantics is more concerned with the specification of invariant, stable meanings that can be associated with expressions.

PRAGMATIC PRESUPPOSITION

Because presuppositions are not invariant and they are not stable, they became an ideal unit of linguistic analysis for pragmaticists. Earlier pragmatic theories of presupposition offered little more than possible definitions for the concept using pragmatic notions (Gazdar 1979:103ff offers a list of these definitions and a discussion). Despite their differing terminology, these definitions have been subsumed by Levinson (1983: 204–205) into two basic concepts: (a) appropriateness (or felicity), and (b) mutual knowledge (or common ground, or joint assumption) indicated as follows:

31. An utterance A pragmatically presupposes a proposition B iff A is appropriate only if B is mutually known by participants.

Levinson, however, argues that the utility of the notion of appropriateness is objectionable and that the mutual knowledge condition is far too strong. He supports Gazdar's (1979:105) suggestion that what one presupposes is consistent with the propositions assumed in the context (Levinson 1983:205).

Consequently, an earlier definition of pragmatic presupposition by Stalnaker (1974) is still prevalent today. He defines this concept in the following way:

32. A proposition **P** is a pragmatic presupposition of a speaker just in case the speaker assumes or believes that **P**, assumes or believes that his addressee assumes or believes that **P**, and assumes or believes that his addressee recognized that he is making these assumptions (Stalnaker 1974:200).

Stalnaker's definition suggests that, unless they explicitly object, participants in a discourse implicitly accept the presuppositions of the utterances of other participants. Consequently, the addressee's failure to object to infelicitous presuppositions would violate Grice's maxim of quantity, which calls for a participant's contribution to a discourse be as informative as required for the purpose of communication (for more on this maxim, refer to Grice 1957).

In a later study, Stalnaker (1978) discerns two types of discourse contexts: defective and non-defective. The former contexts, according to Stalnaker, are inherently unstable and necessarily result in efforts to equilibrate the "context sets" of participants. The latter contexts, Stalnaker suggests, are the "context sets," or the possible worlds that speakers take to be live options, which do not vary from participant to participant.

At a pragmatic level of analysis, then, the defeasibility problem in presupposition can be overcome by employing linguistic procedures that represent textual contents calling for access to the lexical properties of terms, the previously represented contents in the discourse context itself, and the deictic context of utterances. But this still leaves unsolved the projection problem in presupposition.

Fortunately, Gazdar (1979) provides potential analysts with a set of procedures that correctly predict the defeat of presuppositions, even in cases where presuppositional compositionality fails to hold. Gazdar suggests that one identifies all the possible presuppositions of a sentence, no matter the defeasibility or projection concerns. Once the actual assertion is represented, one can then enter its entailments, followed by its conversational implicatures. Only then can one employ a canceling mechanism to determine the plausible presuppositions, eliminating those presuppositions that are logically inconsistent with the discourse as represented. Whatever survives is then added to the representation. In essence, an analyst must mark the representations of presuppositions so that they can be retracted if, later in the discourse, they are contradicted by assertional contents.

Gazdar's procedures are framed in terms of the individual speaker. Put differently, the actual presuppositions are those members of the set of possible presuppositions that are consistent with what a speaker has previously asserted, entailed, implicated, and presupposed. Levinson (1983:212n) suggests that Gazdar's procedures can be extended to what discourse participants jointly presume, as called for by Stalnaker's definition of pragmatic presupposition quoted in (32).

CONTEXTS OF THE DISCOURSES OF THE THREE NATIONAL ANTHEMS

The story behind the African national anthem requires retelling. The South African Enoch Mankayi Sontonga composed what later became the African national anthem, "Nkosi Sikelel' iAfrika," in 1897. This song was composed at a time when Africans in South Africa were living in a period of high political expectation. The song is a product of the politico-religious movement of the time, which took the form of the religion of the oppressed, and became the ideological expression of the progressive tendencies of the anti-colonial resistance (Meli 1988:32).

The composer, Sontonga, who was born in Lovedale, Cape Province, in 1860, left school at an early age and went to live in Johannesburg. A devout Christian endowed with a wonderful voice, Sontonga wrote both words and music to the song. "Nkosi Sikelel' iAfrika" was publicly sung for the first time in 1899 at the ordination of the Reverend M. Bowemi, a Methodist minister. The occasion was said to have been marked with joy, but the composition itself was inspired by a somewhat melancholy strain: Africans were far from being happy at the height of the Anglo-Boer War (Meli 1988:32).

Sontonga died in 1904, but African teachers and poets such as J. L. Dube (who later became the African National Congress [ANC] president-general), R. T. Caluza, and S. E. K. Mqhayi popularized the song. The song was originally intended as a hymn, but people started singing it in schools and churches in all provinces and developed an adaptation acknowledging the unity of the African people. On January 8, 1912, it was sung at the birth of the ANC; and in 1925, the ANC adopted it as its national anthem. Today, adapted forms of the song serve as national anthems for Namibia, Tanzania, Zambia, and Zimbabwe (Meli 1988:32–33).

The Jamaican national anthem was written in 1962 to commemorate the country's independence from Great Britain. The Hon. the Rev. Hugh B. Sherlock, OJ, OBE, JP, DD, LLD, MIBA, wrote the lyrics to the anthem and the Hon. Robert Charles Lightbourne, OJ, wrote the music (Jamaican Government Public Relations Office n.d., n.p.).

Sherlock was minister of religion, served as a consultant for the Intercontinental Biography, served as chairman of Boys Town All-Age, and served as chairman of Boys Town Finance Committee. Born in Portland, Jamaica, on March 21, 1905, he was the son of the late Rev. Terrence M. Sherlock and Adina Trotter-Sherlock. He was educated at Beckford and Smith's

School, Calabar High School, Caenwood Methodist Theological College in Jamaica, and was ordained in 1937 (Jamaican Government Public Relations Office n.d.:228).

Lightbourne was chairman and managing director of Textiles of Jamaica, Ltd., and served as vice president of the Jamaican Olympic Association. Born in Morant Bay, Jamaica, on November 29, 1909, he was the son of the late Robert Augustus Lightbourne, minister and politician. He was educated at Jamaica College and in England (Jamaican Government Public Relations Office n.d.:181).

The period in which the Jamaican national anthem was written was one of hardship for the country. Jamaica faced a high inflation rate, a high unemployment rate, and massive poverty. Many citizens were dissatisfied, and their discontent sometimes led to riots and violent crime. Some Jamaicans supported Black Power groups that called for more African Jamaican control over the economy and the government. The Black Power groups also urged the government to nationalize the bauxite and alumina industries, which were largely controlled by foreign companies (Singham and Singham 1976:11:23).

Lift Ev'ry Voice and Sing was written in 1901 by James Weldon Johnson (1871-1938). He was a novelist, playwright, and poet (Brooks 1984:179). He pursued his studies through a collegiate course and emerged as a major voice in public affairs and one of the major authors of his time. Johnson served as Spence Professor of Creative Literature at Fisk University. He translated the libretto of Enrique Granados' opera, Goyescas, which was written by Fernando Periquet, from Spanish to English to be presented at the Metropolitan Opera House in New York (Cuney-Hare 1936/1974:167, 169).

Johnson inaugurated New York's Harlem Renaissance movement with the publication of his *Fifty Years and Other Poems* in 1917. The movement, which became the centerpiece of African American intellectual life, was an outcome of the disillusionment of African Americans concerning their plight in the United States after World War I. They became increasingly aware that the democracy for which they had fought and some of their brothers had died in Europe did not exist for them in America. Thus, they became more militant and more articulate in expressing their displeasures about their economic and social conditions (Brooks 1984:203).

Between 1901 and the late 1920s, "Lift Ev'ry Voice and Sing" had emerged as a national patriotic hymn sung for African Americans. It was greatly appreciated for its melodically beautiful production and tremendous racial and national appeal, and was widely used by African American organizations all over the United States (Cuney-Hare 1936/1974:169).

However, from the 1930s to the early 1950s, African American colleges discouraged the singing of what was long regarded as the Negro national hymn, "Lift Ev'ry Voice and Sing." As Branch (1988:137–38) has pointed out, a few African American college presidents even forbade the singing of the hymn. At some institutions, teachers, students, and administrators objected to the inclusion of the spirituals in the repertoires of their college choirs. The reason for this, according to Branch, was that many of the African American teachers and administrators had received their graduate training at White Northern universities. Therefore, the thrust of the educational programs of the colleges was toward preparing students to eventually take their "rightful places" in the mainstream of American culture. As a result, most members of the college communities, including the students, felt that the proper avenue for entering the mainstream was assimilation into White culture.

In sum, the three national anthems were written by Africans who were brilliant, religious, spiritual, and had a positive worldview, despite their travails and those of their people. All three anthems were written during very trying times for the people of the African diaspora.

ANALYSIS: PRESUPPOSITIONS OF THE ANTHEMS

The three anthems read as follows:

African National Anthem

Nkosi Sikelel'i Afrika
Maluphakanisw' upondo lwayo
Yizwa imitandazo yetu
Usi—sikelele

Sikelel' amadol' asizwe
Sikelela kwa nomlisela
Ulitwal' ilizwe ngomonde
Uwusikilele

Sikelel' amalinga etu
Awonanyana nokuzaka
Awemfundo nemvisiswano
Uwasikelele
Woza Moya! [Yihla] Moya!
Woza Moya Oyingcwele!

God bless Africa
Raise up her spirit
Hear our prayers
And bless us

Bless the leaders
Bless also the young
That they may carry the land with patience
And that you may bless them

Bless our efforts
To unite and lift ourselves up
Through learning and understanding
And bless them

Come Spirit! [Descend] Spirit!
Come, Holy Spirit!

Jamaican National Anthem

Eternal Father bless our land,
Guard us with Thy Mighty Hand
Keep us free from evil powers,
Be our light through countless hours.
To our Leaders Great Defender,
Grant true wisdom from above.
Justice, Truth be ours forever,
Jamaica, Land we love.
Jamaica, Jamaica, Jamaica land we love.

Teach us true respect for all,
Stir response to duty's call,
Strengthen us the weak to cherish,
Give us vision lest we perish.
Knowledge send us Heavenly Father,
Grant true wisdom from above.
Justice, Truth be ours forever,
Jamaica, land we love.
Jamaica, Jamaica, Jamaica land we love.

Negro National Anthem

Lift ev'ry voice and sing Till earth and heaven ring, Ring with the harmonies of liberty; Let our rejoicing rise High as the listening skies, Let it resound loud as the rolling sea. Sing a song full of the faith that the dark past has taught us, Sing a song full of the hope that the present has brought us, Facing the rising sun of our new day begun Let us march on till victory is won.

Stony the road we trod, Bitter the chastening rod, Felt in the days when hope unborn had died. Yet with a steady beat, Have not our weary feet Come to the place for which our fathers sighed? We have come over a way that with tears has been watered, We have come, treading our path through the blood of the slaughtered, Out from the gloomy past, Till now we stand at last Where the white gleam of our bright star is cast.

God of our weary years, God of our silent tears, Thou who hast brought us thus far on the way; Thou who hast by Thy might Led us into the light, Keep us forever in the path, we pray. Lest our feet stray from the places, our God, where we met Thee, Lest our hearts drunk with the wine of the world, we forget Thee; Shadowed beneath Thy hand, May we forever stand. True to our God, True to our native land.

It is quite evident from the text of the African National Anthem that all the presupposition triggers[9] in that text are performative verbs/predicates or what Karttunen (1973:174) refers to as plugs: bless, raise up, hear, carry, unite, lift up, and come/descend. From the Jamaican national anthem, it can be seen that all the presupposition triggers are also performatives: bless, guard, keep free, be, grant, love, teach, stir, strengthen, give, and send. What is common to these verbs is that they are used to report on what illocutionary acts (in the sense of Austin 1962) are to be performed. As Karttunen (1973:174) observes, one can report that a certain illocutionary act has taken place (in the texts of the African national anthem and the Jamaican national anthem, that certain illocutionary acts are to take place) without thereby committing oneself to the presuppositions of whatever was said or written on that occasion. For all the stretches of discourses in the texts of these two anthems (the African and the Jamaican), then, the complement sentences have presuppositions which are not presuppositions for the main sentences. (It is assumed here that infinitival and gerundive clauses originate as complete sentences in the underlying syntactic representation. Nothing important hinges on this assumption, as Karttunen correctly points out.)

From the Negro national anthem, several types of presupposition triggers can be identified. However, the majority of these are performatives: lift, ring, let rise, let resound, sing, keep, come, pray, stray, forget, and stand true.

A significant number of the presupposition triggers are factives: facing, trod, felt, out, led, drunk, and is won. Factive verbs/predicates as presupposition triggers carry along the writer's propositions that the complement sentences of the statement represent true propositions. Automatic recognition of such propositions presents no particular problem, as syntactic triggers (the presence of undefeated factive predicates) plainly appear in the pertinent statements in the text of the Negro national anthem.

Many of the presupposition triggers are definite descriptions: the dark past, the present, our new day, the chastening rod, steady beat, our weary feet, our bright star, God of our weary years, thy might, and our hearts. As presupposition triggers, definite descriptions, according to Russell (1905), have nothing like the simple logical translation that we might imagine. Although they occur in natural language as subjects, in logical form they are not logical subjects at all but correspond instead to conjunctions of propositions. Thus, by virtue of the Russellian expansion of the phrases from which this type of propositions are embedded, it can be asserted that the writer of the Negro national anthem noticed, for example, that "there was a dark past" and "there is a present (time)."

A small number of the presupposition triggers are change-of-state predicates: have come, and has brought. Change-of-state predicates as presupposition triggers appear in conditionals, which have all the presuppositions that their antecedents and consequents have independently. This signifies that the author of the Negro national anthem did not want to commit himself to certain false beliefs for which he had no concrete evidence. In semantic terms, the bivalence of a sentence does not depend on whether the proposition of the complement is true.

Thus, the following presuppositions can be derived from the text of the African National Anthem:

33. God blesses, raises up spirits, and listens.
34. The young carry the land.
35. Unity and lifting up oneself hinge on learning and understanding.
36. Spirits come/descend.

From the text of the Jamaican National Anthem, the following presuppositions can be suggested:

37. God blesses, guards, keeps people free, serves as a light, grants true wisdom to leaders, teaches, stirs responses, strengthens the weak, gives vision, and sends knowledge.
38. Utterers want justice and truth.
39. Jamaicans are loving people.

For the Negro National Anthem, many presuppositions can be suggested as follows:

40. There are many voices.
41. There is an earth and a heaven.
42. Liberty is harmonious.
43. There is rejoicing.
44. There are listening skies.
45. There is a rolling sea.
46. There is a song full of faith.
47. There was a dark past.
48. There is a song full of hope.
49. There is a present time.
50. There is a rising sun.
51. There is a new day.
52. Victory can be won.

53. There was a road.
54. There was a chastening rod.
55. There was no hope.
56. There was a steady beat.
57. Utterers' feet were weary.
58. There was a place where utterers' fathers sighed.
59. There were tears.
60. There was blood of the slaughtered.
61. There was a gloomy past.
62. There was a bright star.
63. There is a God.
64. There is a way.
65. God has might.
66. There was light.
67. There is a path.
68. There were places God was met.
69. Utterers have hearts.
70. There is the wine of the world.
71. Utterers can forget God.
72. God has a hand.
73. Utterers have a God.
74. Utterers have a native land.

In sum, 42 presuppositions are identified in the texts of the three national anthems: four in the African National Anthem, three in the Jamaican National Anthem, and 35 in the Negro National Anthem. The break down of these propositions in terms of their types of presupposition triggers are presented in Table 1.

Table 1: Presupposition Triggers in the Three National Anthems

Type of Trigger	African National Anthem		Jamaican National Anthem		Negro National Anthem	
	N	%	N	%	N	%
Change of State Predicates	-	-	-	-	3	8%
Factive Predicates	-	-	-	-	9	26%
Performative Predicates	4	100%	3	100%	14	40%

Definite Descriptions	-	-	-	-	9	26%
Total	**4**	**100%**	**3**	**100%**	**35**	**100%**

As the data for the types of presupposition triggers for the texts of the three national anthems, summarized in Table 1, reveal, the largest proportion of these triggers comprises performative predicates. Reasonably larger proportions of them are factive predicates and definite descriptions; a smaller proportion is made up of change of state predicates.

These presupposition triggers carry propositions of some necessary and sufficient conditions which determine whether the events described in the texts of the three anthems took place. The writers' main statements can thus be looked upon as statements about whether the decisive conditions they (the writers) envisioned for generating the texts were fulfilled, and under what spatial and temporal circumstances.

This is good to know, because these presupposition triggers indicate the sort of range of presuppositional phenomena the authors of the texts had. This set of core phenomena makes it possible for the examination of some further basic properties that the authors' presuppositions exhibit. In essence, while it is important to know the presuppositions of the three national anthems, it is equally important to explore explanations of why the given presuppositions are present in the texts. This will allow for a systematic and empirical analysis of those antecedent factors that are responsible for the suggestions of these presuppositions.

UNDERSTANDING THE PRESUPPOSITIONS IN THE TEXT

The presuppositions identified in the texts of the three national anthems can be grouped within the following content categories in terms of their subject matter:

a. God/Lord: (33), (37), (63), (65), (68), (71), (72), (73).
b. The Young: (34).
c. Unity and Strength: (35).
d. Spirits: (36).
e. Liberty, Justice, and Truth: (38), (42).
f. Love and Joy: (39), (43), (56), (69), (70).
g. Numericalism: (40).
h. Earth and Heaven: (41).
i. Faith and Hope: (46), (48), (51), (52), (53), (62), (64), (66), (67), (74).
j. Ecological Concern: (44), (45), (50).
k. Temporal Sequence: (49).
l. Suffering: (47), (54), (55), (57), (58), (59), (60), (61).

While the presuppositions delineated for the three national anthems are important in knowing the core of the phenomena in the texts, they do not, however, present us with explanations for understanding the anthems. Explanations of the presupposition content categories are, therefore, imperative, because any social scientific endeavor must seek to provide general explanations to "Why?" questions. In this case, why the preceding presupposition categories are evident in the texts examined. When social scientists attempt to explain why a given phenomenon took place, they must provide a systematic and empirical analysis of those antecedent factors in the given situation that made possible the occurrence of that phenomenon.

GOD/LORD

The African notion that God[10] blesses (that is, the gift of divine favor) is derived from the belief of a supreme being as an integral part of the worldview and practiced religion of Africans. The nature of God in African belief is evident from the qualities attributed to him or her. That God is almighty (as the Temne of Sierra Leone say, Kuru Masheba) is one of the most obvious assertions, since supremacy calls for it. As Parrinder (1969:39–40) points out,

> All-powerful is a common name for him (her) and he (she) receives many similar titles: creator, allotter, giver of rain and sunshine, the one who began the forest, the one 'who gives the rots', maker of souls, father (mother) of the placenta, the one who exists by himself (herself). The omnipresence of God, less commonly expressed, is found in sayings such as 'the one who is met everywhere', and 'the great ocean whose head-dress is the horizon'. More clearly God is omniscient: the wise one, the all-seeing, the 'one who brings round the season'. (The feminine attributes in parentheses are mine to indicate that some African cultures have no gender markers for God and some ascribe a feminine gender to God.)

These attributes suggest the transcendence and immanence of God. As such, God is in a position to bless persons, places, things, and ideas.

The African belief that God raises up one's spirit (that is, vivacity, courage, vigor, enthusiasm, etc.) when a person encounters misfortune, sickness, barrenness, quarrels, drought, and any disruption of normal life is manifested in sacrifices of propitiation. Prayers, petitions, and praises all seek augmentation of force by recognizing and invoking the powers of the supreme being. Great endeavors are, therefore, made by Africans to "get up," improve, and modernize their lot to become successful, because they believe that God has not fixed an order that can never change or placed people in positions where they are doomed to stay (Parrinder 1969:72–73).

The sonorous rehearsals of divine qualities attributed to God in African prayers are all geared toward the belief that God listens to them. The Yoruba of Nigeria, for example, begin many prayers with such praise names: Olorun, Olodumare, Baba, Alaanu Julo; God, Almighty, Father, Most Merciful.

Faith in God, however, implies his or her providence. Thus, the poetry of African prayer, delightful as it is in expressive words, is not allowed to deviate from practical purpose. This prayer of the Kikuyu in Kenya is a case in point: "You who make mountains tremble and rivers flood; we offer you this sacrifice so that you may bring us rain. People and children are crying. We beseech you to accept this sacrifice and bring us prosperity" (Parrinder 1969:67–68). All such African prayers are believed to be heard by God who helps his or her suppliant by an intervention, either open or hidden, but powerful and effective.

Before their arrival to the New World, the belief in the existence of God or Lord among those Africans was firmly in place. As Parrinder (1969:39) has observed, the earlier view that African religions were crudely fetishistic, with an idea of God where the deity existed being an importation, has long been replaced by the view that most Africans have had the belief in a supreme being as an integral part of their worldview and practiced religion long before the arrival of the White man. Missionaries found, often to their surprise, that they did not need to convince Africans about the existence of God, or faith in a life after death, for both these fundamentals of world religions were deeply rooted in Africa before their arrival.

The nature of God in African belief was evident from the qualities attributed to him or her. That God is almighty is one of the most obvious assertions, since supremacy calls for it (Parrinder 1969:39).

For Africans, God possessed the power to heal mental and physical illness. God resided in heaven and was the creator of everything on earth: the sun, moon, sky, air, water, plants, humans, animals, etc. God was perceived as the benevolent mother or father, who rewarded goodness but ruthlessly punished evil. God knew all, saw all, and was both omnipotent and omnipresent (Hull 1972:131).

In America, Gullah African Christianity was a vital folk religion, filled with patterns of beliefs linking worshipers with their traditional past. The original Gullah interpretation of religion included treating spirituality as a means of communal harmony, solidarity, and accountability. These features of an African worldview, an African theory of being, and some African customs sometimes superseded or sometimes coexisted with the Christian influence. This was consonant with the notion that in a cohesive and integrated society, each member had a place (Holloway 1990:71).

For the Gullah, God, personified as Jesus, and an African worldview offered them an explanation for life and provided a model of virtue. This belief inspired them to hold on to their faith that freedom on earth would come to them in their progeny (Holloway 1990:71).

In St. Augustine, Florida, African religious patterns exerted continuing influence among African Americans as African naming practices persisted during the era of British control (1763–1784). Another characteristic of black religious life in Florida was the high emotionalism prevalent in traditional African worship (Holloway 1990:101, 111).

In Jamaica, Kumina, regarded as the most African of Jamaican religions, was carried there by a large number of free Africans who arrived there from the 1840s to the 1860s. Many of them settled in St. Thomas, where the religion is the strongest. A religion of Bantu origin, Kumina has been shown to be largely Ki-Kongo in present day Republic of Congo (Senior 1983:91).

THE YOUNG

To prepare African youths to take their places in family life, community affairs, and government, African children mingle with adults in the beginning of their lives, sharing in ceremonies and feasts at home, in working the fields and visiting the markets, and in watching tribunals and funerals. Traditionally, many African societies were divided into age grades, and in adolescence the grade would pass through common ceremonies and initiations (such as the Poro for boys and Sande for girls in Sierra Leone and Guinea, and Kumina in Jamaica) into adulthood.

As Vlahos (1967:192–93) notes, the system of age grouping was one means for organizing large numbers of people from different areas. For various Nilotic tribes, age grouping represented the beginning of government beyond pure family rule. Among the Zulu and Swazi of southern Africa, age grouping served as a military complex from which government is formed. Among the Kikuyu, age grouping was the system of the whole government. Its leaders were selected not by birth, not by election, not even by divine appointment. Instead, Kikuyu leaders were chosen by the accumulation of birthdays. In a government formed by "committee," every Kikuyu could hope to stand at least once in the limelight and, with his "committee" members, to orchestrate communal policy.

Politics in such a fundamental situation, according to Awoonor (1990:3), defined duties and responsibilities alongside obligations and rights. This survival concept is ever-changing, continuing, and dialectical.

UNITY AND STRENGTH

That the prerequisites of unity and strength to lift up oneself in Africa hinge on one's ability to learn during his or her youth from playmates and living with them is hardly a matter of dispute. The Nyakyusa of Tanzania, for instance, once lived in three villages in one: a village for family persons, a village for the persons who ran things, and a village for their children, who were learning to be adults (Vlahos 1967:210).

The Nyakyusa used to divide their interests and activities almost equally between farming and herding. A boy began taking his father's cattle to pasture when he turned six. He did not go out alone, but in a small troop of boys his own age and a little older. Cooking their own food, wrestling and fighting to see which one was the strongest, the Nyakyusa youths acknowledged the leader of all, the one whose order would be followed. When the Nyakyusa boy came home to his mother's meal, he brought his friends along; like a swarm of locusts, they descended on one mother's larder after another (Vlahos 1967:202). The case of the Nyakyusa typifies the closeness and dependence of African youths on one another—because even in a time of change, they still value above all things the togetherness of comradeship and harmony.

African Americans were (and continue to be) quite strong in order to survive. They had to endure political, social, and economic intimidation, supplemented by violence and the threat of violence. As discussed earlier and to be discussed again later, they were the victims of violence even before they began to participate in the political process. The violence intensified during the Reconstruction era. Terrorist organizations like the Ku Klux Klan, the Knights of the White Camelia, the Pale Faces, the White Line, the Knights of the Rising Sun, the White Brotherhood, the Red Shirts, and many others whipped and murdered African Americans and their White sympathizers.

As early as the presidential campaign of 1868, Whites in the Louisiana parishes of Opelousas, Caddo, and Bouvier systematically "hunted down" and killed over 400 African Americans within a month. Later that year in Moore County, North Carolina, the Ku Klux Klan murdered an African American woman and all five of her children while in the process of terrorizing African Americans and White Republicans. The violence was so widespread that Congress was moved to pass the Enforcement Acts of 1870 and 1871 to crush it (Arnold Taylor 1976:25).

Having occurred in the North during the Civil War, race riots became rampant throughout America. The South saw its share of race riots beginning with the era of Reconstruction, in order to keep the African American population cowed and subordinate. Riots occurred in New Orleans and Memphis as early as 1866: in the former city, the riots were caused by White resentment of African American demands for suffrage; in the latter city, the rescue of an African American male by a group of African American soldiers from the custody of the police led to the riot. Other major riots included those in Meridian, Mississippi, in 1871; in Savannah, Georgia, in 1872; and in Hamburg and Charleston, South Carolina, in 1876. African Americans in Charleston, however, angry over many indignities, became the aggressors (Arnold Taylor 1976:25).

African American resistance to and retaliation against violence directed at them were commonplace. Groups of African Americans responded by patrolling the streets of Wilmington, North Carolina, for four days, armed with such weapons as guns and fence rails when the Conservative White press and other elements in the city attempted to create a scare in April 1868. The purpose was to discourage blacks from voting on the drafted state constitution. This demonstration forced the Ku Klux Klan to disappear from the Wilmington area for the remainder of the Reconstruction period. During the same month, a group of about 200 African Americans in Alexandria, Louisiana, armed with clubs, routed Klansmen who had been parading throughout the community threatening to kill any African American who dared to vote on that state's constitution. Also, on the night of July 4, 1868, between 20 to 30 African Americans in Columbia, Tennessee (where the Ku Klux Klan was quite entrenched), attacked a group of about 250 Klan members (Arnold Taylor 1976:25–26).

Between the end of Reconstruction and the inauguration of apartheid, African Americans continued to resist or retaliate against White violence. Democratic fraud at the polls also occasionally evoked a violent reaction from African Americans. However, physical atrocities against African Americans, such as beatings and lynching, provoked African American resistance and retaliation more than fraud at the polls or other forms of White chicanery. Such crimes by Whites moved even the relatively conservative African American leaders to endorse violent responses (Arnold Taylor 1976:62–63).

During the 20th century, many African American leaders endorsed the principle of individual and collective use of violence in self-defense. For example, on many occasions between 1905 and 1935, W. E. B. Du Bois endorsed not only the use of violence in self-defense, but prophesied a war between the races. Nevertheless, even the more moderate James Weldon Johnson, while rejecting the use of violence as a weapon to dismantle the racial order, declared in 1934 that faced with mob violence, African Americans must give up their lives to resist it. In 1925, the National Association for the Advancement of Colored People (NAACP) argued and won the same principle in the Ossian Sweet case (Arnold Taylor 1976:63).

By the 1950s, militant self-defense became as much a part of the African American protest tradition as demonstrations, boycotts, litigation, petitions, and appeals to Americans' sense of justice. The willingness of Robert Williams of Monroe, North Carolina, in the late 1950s and the Deacons for Defense in Louisiana in the 1960s to take up arms to defend their African American communities reflected an impulse that was deeply rooted in the African American Southern experience (Arnold Taylor 1976:65).

From the landing of the first enslaved Africans in Jamestown, Virginia, in August of 1619, one year before the Mayflower's arrival, until their freedom was finally granted, 250 years elapsed. African Americans were able to survive these 250 years of anxiety, frustration, and hardship because of their mental and physical stamina that would not permit the concession of defeat.

The history of the skillful and resilient Captain Cudjoe, who worked to unite his fellow Maroons to resist Spanish and English domination in Jamaica, is well documented. Cudjoe was a member of a group of runaway slaves who roamed the Clarendon hills (near Cave Valley) in the 17th century. He emerged as the leader and welded together all the Clarendon Maroon bands. So great did his fame become that many Maroons made their way from other parts of Jamaica to serve under his leadership (Senior 1983:91).

SPIRITS

In order to understand the idea behind the presupposition that spirits[11] come or descend, it is important to begin by discussing the notion of spirits within the African context. Gods and ancestors are regarded generally as divinity or spiritual activity. However, for Africans, these terms do not suggest a separateness from man, or an opposition of spiritual and material, or sacred and secular. Instead, gods are regarded as being dependent on the supreme being, and that all powers, divine and human, are interrelated. In essence, even humans are considered spirits (Parrinder 1969:47).

Many African myths thus suggest that after creating the world and living here in olden days, God retired to the heavens where she or he is now. In order to solicit God's help, then, people must summon them to come/descend.

The Yoruba say that Olorun, "owner of the sky," lives in heaven with other divinities. Below was a waste marsh with no solid ground, where divinities came down to play and hunt. The Mende of Sierra Leone say that God was formerly nearer to humans than now, and gave them everything they requested. But humans troubled God so often that God decided to go far away into the heavens. Similar themes have been documented to exist in Ivory Coast, Ghana, Togo, Dahomey, Nigeria, Sudan, Burundi, Zambia, Zaire, and Kenya (Parrinder 1969:30–33). The presupposition that spirits come or descend hinges, thus, on the notion of the creation and the separation of humans and God.

For members of the Kumina religion in Jamaica, singing, dancing, and drumming are the three most important elements in their sessions. The drums are the most important for the controls they exercise over certain kinds of spirits. Leaders have to serve long apprenticeships before attaining the highest position in the group. Leaders can be women or men. The spirits are originally of three ranks: sky gods, earthbound gods, and ancestral spirits.

LIBERTY, JUSTICE, AND TRUTH

As Spencer (1990:35–44) has suggested, no other sentiment has inspired African Americans to exalted strains as the love of liberty. He added that there existed among African Americans a deep consciousness of the injustices of slavery and a due appreciation of the blessings of freedom, which gave rise to many antislavery songbooks.

Witvliet (1987) also has argued that the history of the African American struggle for liberation is deeply rooted in the belief that one's own liberation is related to that of the other. This notion, he pointed out, is evident from the following spiritual:

> You say the Lord has set you free, ...
> Why don't you let yo' neighbour be! (Witvliet 1987:18)

An examination of a number of historical records reveals that a variety of approaches were utilized by African Americans to free a fortunate minority of the enslaved from bondage. Manumission, escape, and philanthropy were all used in efforts to secure liberty for enslaved individuals and their families (see, for example, the many stories in Foner 1970).

Many of the enslaved received their liberty through military and naval service in the colonial wars and the American Revolution. Another source of freedom was self-purchase. Generally, the enslaved who were able to buy their liberty used their special trade skills to hire themselves out. Some obtained their monies to buy their freedom in unique ways: the self-taught George Moses Horton sold his love lyrics to students at the state university of North Carolina; Denmark Vesey and Newport Gardner used their winnings from the Rhode Island lottery—the former in

1782, the latter in 1791; James Derham, a male nurse, medical assistant, and apothecary in New Orleans saved money from his services to buy his freedom in 1783, becoming an outstanding physician within six years. Derham then moved to Philadelphia, repeated his success, and won the respect of his colleagues in the medical profession (Quarles 1964:83–85).

Still, other enslaved Africans sought liberty through rebellion, albeit not always successfully. For example, five slaves joined John Brown and 14 of his followers in their attempt to seize a government arsenal in Harpers Ferry in northwestern Virginia. Brown's plan failed mainly because it was staged in an area where there were few enslaved Africans and had given them no foreknowledge of his plan of attack. Consequently, Brown and his 21 men were captured and executed, leading the soldiers in blue to sing "John Brown's Body" (Quarles 1964:108). In 1793, when African-born Angolans rose up against their Carolina masters, slaves from that region were no longer so desirable. Also, a nonimportation act was put in effect for ten years following the 1793 Stono Rebellion (Holloway 1990:69). The three greatest slave revolts in American history occurred within the space of 31 years during the 19th century. The first was led by a 24-year-old enslaved Virginian, Gabriel, in 1800. Gabriel devised a plan for three columns of armed slaves to attack Richmond, seize the arsenal, and kill all the Whites, except for Quakers, Methodists, and Frenchmen. Before Gabriel could regroup, the militia had been alerted, and he and 25 of his men were captured and executed. Denmark Vesey, a slave carpenter in Charleston who won enough money in a lottery to buy his freedom, began organizing for an armed insurrection among the enslaved in Charleston and the surrounding countryside. However, Vesey's plot was betrayed by a privileged enslaved African, leading to Vesey's execution. Nat Turner's rebellion occurred 10 years after Vesey was executed. Turner's uprising was the last major revolt that got beyond the planning stage. He had no grand plan, and started out with only a handful of followers. His life revolved around religion, conducting religious services among the enslaved in Southampton County, Virginia. Between 1828 and 1830, Turner saw visions and spirits, which he interpreted as divine instructions to lead the slave revolt. Turner and his men killed about 60 Whites before being captured and killed (Foner 1970:113–15).

The Gullah especially were extremely courageous. Their men, women, and children risked their lives in the pursuit of freedom when the Union Army occupied part of South Carolina. They did not only survive, they taxed their creative talents to develop their own community (Holloway 1990:76).

In their call for total emancipation, African Americans became active participants in newspaper work, owning and managing 24 periodicals during the 30 years after the Civil War (1861–1865). These African American newspapers were not the official mouthpiece of the abolitionist societies, but they fully supported the crusade. Although some encountered financial difficulties, they still managed to publish a few series. The common devotion of these periodicals to the principles of liberty and equality was underscored by some of their titles—*Freedom's Journal, The Rights of All, Mirror of Liberty, Impartial Citizen*, and *Herald of Freedom* (Quarles 1964:106-107).

As John Taylor (1975:398) observed, it is to the enslaved African's credit that s/he refused to lapse into a permanent state of docility; and that even though s/he was occasionally forced to cope with the aggressive feelings toward Whites by means of defense mechanisms, s/he nevertheless determined to use his/her limited resources to seek his/her liberty. This determination, according to Taylor, spilled over into some White people's consciousness and emancipation eventually followed.

JOY AND LOVE

Before they were brought to the shores of the New World, the Africans had expressed themselves musically in all life situations. Likewise, in America and in the Caribbean, the various generations of enslaved Africans used songs to accompany menial labor, learn facts, vent their frustrations, share religion, and relate their life conditions. The song served as a master index to the enslaved African's mind (John Taylor 1975:387).

The enslaved were able to develop a means of ingenious covert expression which was their own through their songs. Using the Judeo-Christian vocabulary, they attached secondary meanings, images, and concepts to the song texts. They were able to harbor and express thoughts indiscernible to outsiders by developing this type of communication. Not understanding what the enslaved were doing, Whites poked fun at them for using such unintelligible jargon. In order to preserve for themselves a degree of intellectual freedom, enslaved Africans endured this ridicule (John Taylor 1975:387).

For example, as Llaila Olela Afrika of Gullah country points out, in 1800, the spiritual "Swing Low, Sweet Harriet" was sang to indicate freedom. Gullah plans to escape were communicated in "time," "place," and "event" cryptic code of gospels when Whites were near. The gospel songs and words were often changed to "Swing Low, Sweet Chariot" when Whites were around. Today, it is sung as "Swing Low, Sweet Chariot" (1989:22).

As John Taylor (1975:389) has pointed out, the "happy songs" were the enslaved's means of making himself happy, not of expressing happiness. Indeed, there was nothing glamorous about being enslaved that could make the individual happy. In fact, many songs openly expressed despair, frustration, and sorrow.

NUMERICALISM

Mazrui (1977:247) has defined "numericalism" as an aspect of intergroup relation describing the collection of attitudes or general principles that assign a moral premium on numerical advantage. He distinguished the range of forms that numericalism manifests—from the moral complexities of "majority rule" to the simple belief that "there is strength in numbers." The two ideas, he added, do not necessarily amount to the same thing, but that they could indeed overlap. The liberal concept of majority rule rests on the idea that those who prevail in numbers are to dominate in politics. The notion of "strength in numbers," on the other hand, could be called upon even in situations in which majority rule as an elaborate system of government is not in favor. Even in situations where the power of numbers is seen in physical terms, numericalism still hinges on the belief that there is dignity in being numerous.

For African Americans, there have been many occasions when the more militant among them saw the significance of their numbers in quasi-military terms. Even during slavery, African American superiority in individual situations occasionally turned an African American's thought toward a possible rebellion. In situations where it did not lead to rebellion, this was sometimes interpreted by African American militants as a sign of servility. A defiant and religious African American who had lived close to slavery in North Carolina, David Walker, for example, put it this way in 1829:

> Here now, in the Southern and Western Sections of this country (United States) there are at least three coloured persons for one white, why is it that those few weak, good-for-nothing whites are able to keep so many able men...in wretchedness and misery? It shows what the blacks are, we are ignorant, abject, servile and mean—and the whites know it—they know that we are servile to assert our rights as men—or they would not fool with us as they do (1829/1965:129).

Walker went on to add:

> O Americans! Americans!! I call God—I call angels—I call men, to witness that your DESTRUCTION is at hand, and will be speedily consummated unless you REPENT (1829/1965:129).

In recent times, the African American population has come to perceive the significance of its size in electoral rather than revolutionary terms. African Americans have come to link their size with the liberating potential of the franchise. The African American historian, Aptheker, for example, captured this sentiment quite well when he stated:

> It never was right 'for the administration' to 'postpone' effective action on the Negro question because of so-called political expediency; to say it is not wrong, it is unwise....President Kennedy would have remained a United States Senator if but 75 per cent of the Negro vote went his way in 1960 rather than the 85 per cent cast for him (1964:109).

A similar observation has been made by contemporary African American leaders about the importance of the African American vote in the (1992) presidential election. Many have asserted that the African American vote made the difference in President Bill Clinton's electoral victory over former President George Bush.

As Mazrui (1977:249) observed, at its more revolutionary peak, the African Americans' belief in the importance of their numbers becomes more astute. Speeches to African Americans suggesting that they reduce their rate of reproduction are widely interpreted as a device to keep them numerically weak. Mazrui also suggested that the battle cry of revolutionary African American militancy might almost be paraphrased in the following slogan: "Burn, baby, burn!--and then breed some more!" This, he believed, is a dual strategy of engaging both in destructive acts, which weaken the power of the White man, and in creative acts, which strengthen the power of the African American. In short order, how can African Americans "lift ev'ry voice and sing" if there are not enough voices to be lifted?

EARTH AND HEAVEN

The notions of earth and heaven (or heaven and earth) were not foreign to Africans before their arrival to the New World. As Parrinder (1969:54), for example, has pointed out, when a grave is dug in the ground a libation is made to the spirit, a custom that was taken to America and other parts of the New World by enslaved Africans. This veneration of the earth by African Americans and Jamaicans, for example, can be traced back to a number of African cultures. Ashanti drummers address the earth in the following words:

Earth, while I am yet alive,
It is upon you that I put my trust …
We are addressing you,
And you will understand (Parrinder 1969:54).

The powers of earth include the spirits of hills and great monuments like Mount Cameroon and Mount Kilimanjaro. Even the small hills in Ibadan, Nigeria, have rituals recording the foundation of the city. A holiday is proclaimed every year when work stops and fires are extinguished until they are relit by the priest who is regarded the "worshiper of the hills." Rocks and outstanding formations are seen as centers where special power is manifested and available (Parrinder 1969:55).

Many Africans believed (and many still do) that the first users of metals descended from heaven with metal weapons and tools to clear the forest. Blacksmithery is still an expert profession, and many smiths serve as priests to the god of metal (Parrinder 1969:56).

Thus, it is not surprising that John Taylor (1975:397) found, after studying earlier African American spirituals, that slaves held the belief of heaven being a dimension of self-extension in the sense of private possession. They believed that in heaven, there will be no proscription, no segregation, no separateness, no slave row. They also believed that there will exist the most psychologically dramatic of all manifestations of freedom: that is, complete freedom of movement.

FAITH AND HOPE

According to John Taylor (1975:392—93), one aspect of self-pity reflected in African American spirituals derived from the enslaved's hope that the tables would eventually be turned on their oppressors. Put differently, the greater the suffering at the hands of the Whites in this life, the greater the victory over them in the afterlife would be. Self-pity was one way for slaves to resolve the crisis, not an end in itself; that although they felt sorry for themselves, and would ask others to pity them as well, they believed that they would not be ultimately defeated.

Another way the enslaved coped with their status was their identification with Jesus—the suffering hero. This identification was valuable to them not only because it helped them explain their position (whether unjust fate, or even the will of God), but also to avoid feelings of personal inferiority. It allowed them to experience vicariously feelings of achievement and adequacy through the figure held in great esteem by members of the master class. Moreover, it helped them divert their hatred and resentment toward their White masters and overseers (John Taylor 1975:393—96).

ECOLOGICAL CONCERN

That the ecological concern present in African American hymns was derived from African belief systems is hardly a matter of dispute. As Mazrui (1977:262) has pointed out, for the African, ecological concern goes beyond mere fascination. It requires an individual to conserve and enrich, to empathize with nature, to see a little of oneself and a little of one's God in personal surroundings. It calls for a totemic frame of reference. In this respect, ecological concern is much more deeply interlinked with fundamental aspects of African belief systems than it is to those of Europeans (Mazrui 1977:262).

Totemism in Africa led groups to identify themselves with objects or other animals. Some clans adopted totemic symbols which established a sense of continuity between nature and man. The belief systems of Africans did not assert a monopoly of the soul for the human species alone: trees, mountains, rivers, etc., all have souls (Mazrui 1977:267).

In America, the Gullah of South Carolina, for example, believed in spirits that include super-humans, animals, and objects without biological life. They applied the African ontology, adapted Christianity and bondage to it, and created a religion that used spirituality as a way of self-preservation and as an important component of community life (Holloway 1990:91). As previously noted, this is also true for members of the Kumina religion in Jamaica.

TEMPORAL SEQUENCE

The temporal sequence found in Jamaican and African American hymns can be traced back to traditional African belief systems. These ideologies link the past with the present and the future so intimately that life and death themselves become points on a continuum rather than opposite sides of the same coin.

Mazrui (1977:270) cited Professor John S. Mbiti as stating that the period after death in certain African traditional belief systems is often divided into two parts: (1) Sasa (the now or the present)—an earlier period of "death within living memory," and (2) Zamani (the long ago)—a later period concerning "death beyond living recollection." As long as the individual is remembered by relatives and friends who knew the deceased in life, and who have survived that person, she or he remains in the Sasa period. As long as the deceased is remembered by name, that person is not completely dead: she or he is a member of "the living dead."

Belief in afterlife was central to traditional African religions. But Africans neither viewed the future world with fear, nor as a place for dispensations of rewards and punishments as Christians do. In this afterlife, there was no sickness, disease, poverty, or hunger. Death was a journey to the spirit world, not a divorce from life or earthly beings. Thus, the Gullah retained their West African initiation experience in their attitude towards death when they were brought to the New World. They attached tremendous significance to death, but showed no apprehension to the prospect of dying. As enslaved Africans, they lived in the presence of death constantly and seemed to feel that the phenomenon was as much a part of living as their continuous travail (Holloway 1990:81–82).

SUFFERING

That no other group of people in the New World has endured as much suffering as African Americans is undisputable. Thus, many African Americans reflected realistically in the spirituals upon the circumstances of their lives; and the suffering of Jesus was the most significant aspect of their identification with him. The scenes of Jesus' crucifixion particularly impressed them (John Taylor 1975:395). However, a full discussion of the suffering African Americans have endured in America would require volumes. What follows, therefore, is only a sampling.

After their capture, the enslaved were taken aboard the slave ship. They were usually shackled by attaching the right wrist and ankle of one to the left wrist and ankle of another. The captives slept without covering on bare wooden floors, which were often constructed of unplaned boards. In rough seas, the skins over the elbows of slaves would wear away to the bare bones (Johnson and Campbell 1981:14).

The journey of the enslaved from West African coasts to the New World is frequently referred to as the Middle Passage: that is, the second leg of the triangular trading voyage between the continents of Europe and Africa, Africa and America, and America and Europe. "Tight packers" were by far the most frequently used for shipping slaves by the mid-18th century. The potential profit on each enslaved person was so great that most captains used every possible space for the storage of human cargo (Johnson and Campbell 1981:13–14).

The discomfort of the densely packed quarters of the slave ships was wretched. The hold of a slave vessel was usually about five feet high. When rigged for "tight packing," another shelf or platform was built in the middle of it, extending six feet from each side of the vessel. Another row of the enslaved was packed on the platform when the bottom of the hold was completely filled. A second platform was usually installed to hold more of the enslaved if there was as much as six feet of vertical space in the vessel. Such arrangements made it impossible for the enslaved to sit upright, since they were left with only about two feet of headroom (Johnson and Campbell 1981:14).

Diseases, death, and suicide plagued almost all voyages. Smallpox, scurvy, various forms of ophthalmia, and flux were the diseases most feared. Many slave ships lost half their "cargoes." For every slave brought to America alive, many others died in warfare, along the treks leading to the West African coast, awaiting shipment, or in crowded and contaminated holds of the slaving vessels. Suicide was common on most voyages. On some vessels, it was epidemic. For example, in 1737, more than a hundred enslaved Africans reportedly jumped overboard from the *Prince of Orange* while the ship was anchored at St. Kitts (Johnson and Campbell 1981:15).

The last leg of the Middle Passage, which took about five weeks, was usually less restrictive. All but a few of the enslaved would be released from their iron shackles and brought to the deck for relief. This practice was not motivated by humanitarian purposes, but rather to prepare the enslaved for the market. The enslaved were given bigger meals and as much water as they could drink if the remaining stock of provisions was sufficient. Some captains would set the last day for limited frolicking in the form of costume party on deck, with the females dancing in the sailors' discarded clothing. At the final destination, the captain was rowed ashore to arrange for the sale of his involuntary passengers (Johnson and Campbell 1981:15).

While in America, the enslaved were considered by their masters as property, as stipulated by law. These enslaved Africans were seen as less human, but still were expected to meet certain standards of behavior: obedience, fidelity, humility, docility, cheerfulness, etc. Those who failed to meet these standards received a variety of punishments ranging from public flogging to death. Absolute power for the master meant absolute dependency for the enslaved (Foner 1970:95).

Even after the Emancipation Proclamation was signed by President Abraham Lincoln on January 1, 1863, the woes of African Americans were far from over. Despite the seductiveness of freedom, many formerly enslaved Africans remained at the homesteads of their former masters. They were inspired not by affection for their old masters, but by the hope of finding some means of livelihood in familiar surroundings or among familiar people. As an assembly of African Americans in Charleston, South Carolina, recognized in the fall of 1865, White prejudice was the major obstacle to real liberty (Arnold Taylor 1976:5–6).

African Americans in Charleston soon learned that not only were Whites in South Carolina disinclined to rise above their deeply ingrained prejudices, but that neither President Lincoln nor his successor, President Andrew Johnson, was in a position to envisage a place of equality and dignity for Africans in American society. Both men believed that America was a "White man's country" and must remain that way. During the course of the Civil War, Lincoln investigated and launched projects aimed at colonizing the Africans in Haiti and other parts of Latin America. Despite his belief that the highly intelligent Africans and those who had fought on the side of the Union should be accorded the right to vote, he made no provisions for extending citizenship rights to freedmen in his plan to restore the Southern states to their "proper place" within the Union. Johnson privately suggested that the right of suffrage be extended to literate and propertied African Americans as a way of facilitating Northern acceptance of his lenient Reconstruction program. However, he was adamantly opposed to elevating the mass of African Americans to civil and political equality in the South. Such a development, according to him, would lead to the dreaded "Africanization" of the region. Encouraged by Lincoln and Johnson's attitudes, Southern states enacted laws ("black codes") in 1865 and 1866 that came close to reinstating the system of slavery (Arnold Taylor 1976:6).

The Lincoln and Johnson administrations supplemented the "black codes" with restriction of suffrage and public education to Whites in order to assure the subordinate status of African Americans. Many towns joined the bandwagon by passing ordinances that severely limited the social, economic, and political freedom of formerly enslaved Africans. Many Southern Whites were not content on legislation alone to keep freedmen in their place. The freedmen, no longer having the status of property and, as a result, no longer enjoying the protection of their former masters against physical abuse by other Whites, became victims of violence. These African Americans were beaten, maimed, and killed; their schools, churches, and personal property were frequently ransacked and burnt (Arnold Taylor 1976:7).

During this era, the Ku Klux Klan was formed and soon emerged as the leading terrorist organization of the Reconstruction period. The activities of this organization, the "black codes," and the denial of suffrage and education to African Americans were widely endorsed by Southern Whites (Arnold Taylor 1976:8).

Freedmen who migrated to the North were not welcomed with open arms either. Northern Whites, who had shown little or no unusual hostility toward African Americans already living in their midst, were not in a mood to welcome those from the South. These newcomers were considered crude and rough. Many Whites living in the West had hoped also to keep their region free not only of slavery, but of freedmen as well (Johnson and Campbell 1981:41).

During the antebellum period, conditions continued to deteriorate for African Americans in the North. Physical and social conditions in the 1830s were so harsh that many were convinced that African Americans would eventually be annihilated. Northern and Western Whites became more hostile as the population of African Americans continued to increase in these areas. On many occasions, the violence culminated in riots. In the 1830s and 1840s, racial riots frequently erupted in New York State, Ohio, and Pennsylvania (Johnson and Campbell 1981:41–42).

As can be gleaned from the presuppositional analysis of the three national anthems, for the African, politics defines duties and responsibilities alongside obligations and rights. All these relate to the various activities that have to do with survival. The survival concept is continuing, dynamic, and dialectical. The fundamental principle that is at the basis of this conception is a moral one.

The African moral order never defined rigid frontiers of good and evil. Good and evil exist in the same continuum. Whatever is good, by the very nature of its goodness, harbors a grain of evil. This is a guarantee against any exaggerated sense of moral superiority that goodness alone may entail. The notion of perfection, therefore, is alien to African thought. Perfection in itself constitutes a temptation to danger, an invitation to arrogance and self-glorification. The principle of balance defines the relationship between good and evil and vice versa.

CHAPTER 8

✟

Conclusion and Suggestion

Those linguists who have established the academic tenet that African American English is systematic and rule-governed are to be commended. My only criticism is that they have tended to sidestep the implication that since our language is systematic and rule governed, since it has grammar, teachers ought to leave it alone. Instead, linguists tend to make pronouncements regarding matters about which they lack expertise. As DeBose (1991:3) cogently observes, they appropriate the role of the job placement specialist and suggest that although African American English is fine, Black folk ought to learn to speak like White people anyhow in order to increase their chances to get good jobs. Black people know full well the costs of survival in an alien world, and the extent to which it potentially involves compromising our very souls, and we do not need White linguists to tell us that White-talking Negroes may fare better in job interviews.

If those linguists who managed to use African American English to advance their careers want to give something back to the African American community, they can start by keeping their advice on how to talk to prospective employers to themselves. They should stick to what they are expert in and proclaim to mainstream society that however Black the English of my sisters and brothers might sound, it's English right on. If they want to give somebody advice on what to do about African American English, they should give it to the teachers who would correct it and the employers who would discriminate against its speakers. They should make it short and plain: Leave it alone! Just leave it alone! And to those African American public figures, such as Jesse L. Jackson, Cornell West, and Kweisi Nfume who believe that White English is superior and African American English is inferior, the saying about them was provided by Ngég« wa Thiong'o as follows: "It is the final triumph of a system of domination when the dominated start singing its virtues." Indeed, African American English, which makes up between 70 and 80 percent of the words and expressions America has thus far contributed to the English language, cannot be "inferior."

From the point of view of linguistics, then, the most satisfactory solution to problems encountered by speakers of African American English in a Standard-American-English–dominated society is the adoption in schools of a combination of the two varieties—a sort of bidialectalism and appreciation of dialect differences, bearing in mind that bidialectalism is likely to be only partially successful (and then probably only in the case of writing), and may be dangerous if insensitively handled, from the point of view of fostering linguistic insecurity. It is the attitudes that should be changed, and not the language. The problem is not really a linguistic one, but a sociopolitical one. Given time, this approach might prove to be simpler, since it may be easier to change attitudes than to alter the native speech patterns of a people. The following empirical evidences seem to support my position.

Reacting to California's Senate Bill 205, which mandates that all pupils in the state become proficient in English, regardless of race, color, or other characteristics by immediately terminating the Standard English Proficiency (SEP) program for speakers of non-SAE varieties, John Rickford wrote an op-ed entitled "S.B. 205—Well-intentioned but uninformed" for the *Los Angeles Times* (March 28, 1997). In the piece, Rickford cites a number of studies done in both the United States and Europe, which show that the goal of mastering the standard variety is more effectively achieved by employing approaches that take the other varieties into consideration than by those that ignore or try to condemn them into nonexistence. He also notes that one effective means of taking the other varieties into account is the contrastive analysis approach which is at the heart of SEP. In this approach, students are explicitly taught to recognize the differences between other varieties and standard features, and then schooled in the standard variety through identification, translation, and response drills. The following are some of the success stories:

a. Hanni Taylor reports in her book, *Standard English, Black English, and Bidialectalism* (1989), that a group of inner-city Aurora University students from Chicago, who were taught with contrastive analysis techniques, showed a 59 percent reduction in the use of Ebonics features in their SAE writing, while students taught by traditional methods showed an 8.5 percent increase in the use of such features.

b. Henry Parker and Marilyn Crist in their book entitled *Teaching Minorities to Play the Corporate Language Game* (1995) report using the bidialectal contrastive approach successfully with speakers of other English varieties in Tennessee and Chicago at preschool, elementary, high school and college levels.

c. The 18-year-old program in De Kalb county, Georgia, where 5th and 6th grade students in eight schools are taught to switch from their "home speech" to "school speech" has proven successful by using contrastive analysis methods. The program won a "Center of Excellence" designation award from the National Council for Teachers of English in

1996, as students who had taken the course had improved their verbal test scores at every school.

4. Tore Osterberg's study, *Bilingualism and the First School Language—An Educational Problem Illustrated by Results from a Swedish Dialect Area* (1961), is about a group of a Swedish variety speakers who were first taught to read and write in their variety and then transitioned to standard Swedish. After 35 weeks, the variety method showed itself superior both in reading speed and comprehension.

e. Tove Bull reports on a similar study done in Norway and published in *Troms Linguistics in the Eighties* (1990), in which he describes the successes of ten classes of Norwegian first graders who were taught to read and write either in their Norwegian varieties or standard Norwegian. Bull's results are similar to those of Osterberg: the non-standard variety children read significantly faster and better, particularly the less bright children.

f. The most similar American experiment is Gary Simpkins, Grace Holt, and Charlesetta Simpkins' *Bridge Readers* (1977), which provide reading materials in Ebonics, a transitional variety, and Standard English. The 417 students across the country taught with Bridge showed an average reading gain of 6.2 months over four months of instruction, while 123 taught by regular methods gained only 1.6 months, reflecting the same below par progress which leads African American and other English varieties speakers to lag behind.

The preceding success stories and the following are mentioned in another paper entitled "Using the Vernacular to Teach the Standard" that Rickford presented at the California State University–Long Beach Conference on Ebonics held on March 29, 1997:

g. One of the most dramatic examples of introducing reading in a non-standard language and then switching to the standard was reported by Pedro Orata in his 1953 study on 14 schools in Iloilo Province in the Philippines. In this study, half of the children were taught completely in English for four grades while the other children were first taught for two years in Hiligaynon, their native Philippine language, and then switched to English. The finding is that the children who began in Hiligaynon very rapidly caught up with and even surpassed those who started in English in subjects ranging from reading to social studies, and even arithmetic. This was a massive study done over a fairly long period: from 1948 to 1954.

Despite their dramatic success, the Bridge Readers were discontinued due to hostile and uninformed reactions to the recognition of Ebonics in the classroom. William Stewart and Joan Baratz's gallant effort to introduce dialect readers in a school in Washington, D.C., in 1969 met a similar fate.

While contrastive analysis and dialect readers are not the only viable approaches to teaching the standard, the empirical evidence overwhelmingly supports the fact that these innovative techniques do succeed. Thus, policy makers who may be well intentioned but decidedly uninformed should not hamstring programs attempting to use these methods to reverse their devastating failure rates with inner-city African American and other nonstandard English varieties speakers.

CHAPTER 9

✦

REFLECTIONS

When comes my moment to untether?
"it's time!" and freedom hears my hail.
I walk the shore, I watch the weather,
I signal to each passing sail.
Beneath storm's vestment, on the seaway,
battling along the watery freeway,
when shall I start on my escape?
It's time to to drop astern the shape
of the dull shores of my disfavour,
and there, beneath your noonday sky,
my Africa, where waves break high,
to mourn for Russia's gloomy savour,
land where I learned to love and weep,
land where my heart is buried deep.

—Alexander Sergeyevich Pushkin (1799-1837)

In this chapter, I present a few reflections that underscore why those of us who are African-centered can rejoice over the persistence of Ebonics, despite the many efforts to kill it. The first reflection deals with the state of African language studies in the United States, and the second is about the state of language deaths. Together, these reflections serve as a reminder that should Ebonics die, we will lose a substantial part of our culture—an erosion of the rites and rhythms of our African life. A language is culture. It contains a history of a people and all the knowledge they have passed down from generation to generation. A profitable question: From dating to mourning, why are the rules becoming so opaque?

THE STATE OF AFRICAN LANGUAGE STUDIES IN THE UNITED STATES

Africa is the home of about 3,000 languages, making it the most multilingual continent in the world. African language influences in other languages around the world also are quite numerous. Yet, this wealth of languages contrasts with the very limited number of those languages being taught and studied. Indeed, African languages have been categorized as the "lesser taught languages." One may measure the irony of such a label in light of the fact that it includes such widely used lingua francas as Amharic, Hausa, Kiswahili, Krio, Lingala, Shona, Yoruba, and Zulu.

Furthermore, many African languages have never been recorded or written down. For some, only their names are known. In an important classification proposed in the 1960s, four main families of African languages were delineated: (1) Afroasiatic, (2) Khoisan, (3) Niger-Congo, and (4) Nilo-Saharan. However, this classification is quite tentative, as it is based on the comparison of a small number of features from these languages that have so far been analyzed.

Today, the global situation is characterized by transitions in different domains—cultural, economic, political, and social. The current political climate in the United States, for example, does not seem very favorable to the development of African language teaching. Indeed, while there are "push" forces (e.g., the "War on Terrorism," the world economic environment, and competition for new markets) that encourage African language learning, there also are "pull" forces (fueled by persistent budget deficits, institutional retrenchment, and growing xenophobia) that would like to restrict African language learning. In this context, we must be innovative in our efforts to encourage the study of African languages and their influences on other languages.

THE STUDY OF AFRICAN LANGUAGES AND LINGUISTICS

The growth of the academic study of African languages and linguistics in the United States has see-sawed since the end of the Second World War in 1945, as federal dollars were invested in training programs so that the United States would be able to cope with post–World War II era challenges. Most of this money went to major research universities. Consequently, the training in and study of African languages that evolved in these institutions were rooted in the historical development of Western language disciplines, the history of race and power, and the hegemonic control over discourse on languages.

That the study of African languages and linguistics has evolved over time is a truism. By and large, this evolution has implications for the desirable content of African language education. What is not so generally recognized is that the evolution of the study of African languages and linguistics may also have implications for the *process* of African language study. The teaching and learning *context* and *process*—as well as the curricular content—teach. Not only *what* is taught but *how* it is taught should be formed with our educational goals clearly in mind.

The essence of the foregoing discussion hinges on the fact that dramatic changes in the contemporary international business landscape have created conditions that offer compelling reasons for a sea change in every country's attitudes toward cross-cultural communication. The reduction of trade barriers and the steady growth of international transactions have created an enormous need for effective communication among different groups of people. Never before has the economic and social well-being of each nation been so linked to its citizens' ability to function effectively in a multilingual environment.

One of the most graphic illustrations of this phenomenon can be seen in the ramifications of trade agreements, such as the General Agreement on Tariffs and Trade (GATT). Many of the pitfalls of this trade agreement for Western nations hinges on the glaring lack of expertise in non-European language skills and cross-cultural competence on the part of Western professionals. Concern about this issue prompted the U.S. Trade Representative's office, in collaboration with the Center for Quality Assurance in International Education (CQAIE), to sponsor a meeting in February of 1995 with a number of service professionals. The purpose of the meeting was to discuss the nature of the American economy in the era of the General Agreement of Trade in Services (GATS), the World Trade Organization (WTO), and the North American Free Trade Agreement (NAFTA).

The transformation of the economies of the major industrialized nations from manufacturing into service economies, both domestically and internationally, has tremendous implications for the communication competence of these countries' professionals. Unlike the sale and transfer of goods, which require personal communication among different parties in the period leading up to a transaction, the sale and provision of services require comprehensive interaction on a regular and ongoing basis. In addition, transactions of goods are usually carried out by a circumscribed number of elites with specialized training, who negotiate agreements and exchange technical information. Such elites can generally be counted on to have a mastery of the major European languages. In contrast, the provision of health care services, for example, implies a setting where the professional is interacting with a broad cross-section of the population. Providers of services must be able to speak the target language with a degree of fluency, and have a basic comprehension of cultural assumptions and norms of the society in which they operate.

As long as much cross-cultural competencies are lacking, it is unlikely that the highly touted trade agreements can achieve the desired effects.

Furthermore, without a deeper comprehension of the linguistic frames of reference of other people, ethnic conflicts and inter-cultural hostilities will continue to breed strife and impede economic growth for all.

It is clear then that the citizens of any nation can no longer afford to be complacent about their inability to comprehend the dimension of another culture when economic competition is increasingly dependent on cross-cultural competence. This climate calls for a redefinition of our commitment to the study of African languages and linguistics in our educational systems. Not only should language programs be prompted more widely, but a shift in emphasis is also necessary. Business and professional leaders must take the lead in calling for a work force well-trained in language and cross-cultural communication skills, and political and educational leaders must orchestrate national campaigns to make the study of African and other non-European languages and cultures a top priority in our educational systems.

THE STATE OF LANGUAGE DEATHS

Two aspects of language death—i.e., when a community shifts to a new language totally so that the old language is no longer used—have interested linguists: the linguistic aspect and the sociolinguistic aspect. The linguistic aspect focuses on the last stage of languages that are in use in a community that undergo interesting alterations in their pronunciation and grammar systems, in some respects reminiscent of pidginization (Dressler 1972). The sociolinguistic aspect is the search for the set of factors that cause people to give up a language in favor of another (Fasold 1984).

As journalist Charles Hanley (1996:15–16) points out, scholars have predicted that 90 percent of human languages (an overwhelming majority of which are in the developing world) may die by the mid-21st century, pushed to oblivion's edge by the spread of English and other "world" languages via media, trade, and migration, and by the pressure of dominant vernaculars in their own homelands. Although language sociologist Joshua Fishman (1964) called attention to language death as a phenomenon worthy of study more than four decades ago, the topic has inspired a relatively small number of studies. Linguists Susan Gal (1979) and Nancy Dorian (1981) are the first to provide widely available monograph-length investigations of language death in a specific community. A number of shorter reports on language death have appeared, but European and North American cases have received most of the attention. While linguist Ralph Fasold (1984) suggests that for the time being we have to be content with these available in-depth studies from Europe and North America, it is suggested here that it would be of great interest to have in-depth studies of the phenomenon (which is accelerating in developing countries) to see what similarities and differences there are compared with the Western nation cases.

A major question here, then, is the following: Why should anyone care about language death? The answer to this question is quite obvious. While most of the threatened languages come up short in the trite and trendy, they nevertheless make up for it with a wealth of words for nature's works, for myths and age-old rites and magic, and a complexity rich enough to turn a linguist's inquiry into a lifetime endeavor. Unfortunately, as Hanley (1996:16) points out, only a thin, underfinanced line of linguists around the world is trying to hold back the tide—or at least document—many of these dying languages.

There is a strong tendency for language death to be attributed to the same causes in study after study. The following are the most frequently-cited causes: migration, either by members of small groups who migrate to an area where their language no longer serves them, or by large groups who 'swamp' the local population with a new language (Tabouret-Keller 1968, 1972; Lewis 1972, 1978; Dressler and Wodak-Leodolter 1977; Lieberson and McCabe 1978; Gal 1979; Dorian 1980; Timm 1980); industrialization and other economic changes (Tabouret-Keller 1968, 1972; Dressler and Wodak-Leodolter 1977; Gal 1979; Huffines 1980; Timm 1980;

Dorian 1981); school language and other government pressures (Dressler and Wodak-Leodolter 1977; Gal 1979; Kahane and Kahane 1979; Dorian 1980; Huffines 1980; Timm 1980); urbanization (Tabouret-Keller 1968; Gal 1979; Timm 1980; Dorian 1981); higher prestige for the language being shifted to (Denison 1977; Gal 1979; Kahane and Kahane 1979; Dorian 1981); and a smaller population of speakers of the language being shifted from (Lieberson and McCabe 1978; Kahane and Kahane 1979; Dorian 1981; Huffines 1980). However, there has been very little success in using any combination of these sociological factors to predict when language death will occur. In fact, a number of linguists have reached considerable consensus that we do not know how to predict language death (Kloss 1966, Denison 1977, Gal 1979, Dorian 1981, to name some). Although many of the most often-cited sociological factors are present when language death takes place, it is all too easy to find cases in which some speech community is exposed to the very same factors, but has maintained its language.

Thus, it is suggested here that the aforementioned sociological factors for language death are outcomes of a larger phenomenon—i.e., the world order. Therefore, a major objective of this reflection is to offer a theoretical model, which will demonstrate the relationship between the aforementioned sociological factors, the new world order, and accelerated language deaths in the developing world.

A THEOREM OF ACCELERATED LANGUAGE DEATHS

Since the significance of accelerated language deaths in developing countries is doubly contextual in being both *context shaped* (its contribution to ongoing sequence of linguistic actions cannot adequately be understood except by reference to the context in which it occurs) and *context renewing* (the character of linguistic actions is directly related to the fact that they are context shaped—the context of a next linguistic activity is repeatedly renewed with every current action), *context* then helps an analyst to rule out unintended activities and suppress misunderstandings of certain activities that take place in a linguistic community. In essence, those factors identified as contextual must be those that determine accelerated language deaths in developing countries in actual global activities. In order to explain the concept of accelerated language deaths, the following theoretical framework outlines a model with three different levels of structure. The subsequent discussion explicates these structures.

Sociological Factors:
Migration
Industrialization
School language
New World Order = Urbanization = **Accelerated Language Deaths**
Prestige
Smaller Population

Figure 4: Accelerated Language Deaths: A Theoretical Framework

Proposition: Linguistic domains involve conceptually distinct local contexts for each linguistic transaction. It is these contexts to which linguistics provides a pathway; thus, these contexts are the ones a language analyst can discover through analyzing the uses of languages.

NEW WORLD ORDER

According to foreign policy scholars James Blight and Aaron Belkin (1993:715), the popularity of the concept "New World Order" can be traced to President George Bush's proclamation in his 1991 State of the Union address, when he stated that "we have before us the long-held promise of a New World Order." Blight and Belkin point out that like Presidents Woodrow Wilson and Harry S. Truman before him, Bush sought to build a stable, lawful peace on the foundation of military victory. However, Blight and Belkin argue, far short of a New World Order, new orderliness would be salutary in the chaotic, unipolar confusion of the immediate post–Cold War era. Thus, for them, the demise of the Soviet Union has led certain developing countries to export domestic chaos and engage in violent activities at home.

For economist Haider Khan (1997:1), the so-called "Washington Consensus" ("a complex array of policy reforms underway in the developing countries"), which emerged at the end of the Cold War, seems to be dictating much of the current policy gestures toward third world countries. These indebted countries are forced to swallow the bitter medicine of structural adjustment, regardless of their economic and human conditions. The direct and indirect costs of these policies on the vulnerable groups are already evident, according to Khan.

In the area of foreign language study, for example, the effects are already evident. As linguist Omar Ka (1995:92–93) observes, foreign language study, which has traditionally depended greatly on funding from the U.S. Department of Education through Title VI Foreign Language and Area Studies programs and from the U.S. Agency for International Development, is increasingly threatened in the new political order represented by the Republican majority in the U.S. Congress. In the name of "leaner" government, federal programs, agencies, and even entire departments (such as the Department of Education itself) are either experiencing painful budget cuts. or are in danger of being simply abolished.

As international relations professor Richard Falk (1993) also notes,

> the ending of the Cold war both ended an era of ideological rivalry and stripped away the illusion of consensus about the shape and direction of world order. Beyond the domain of Cold War truisms that have prevailed between 1945 and 1989, there were increasingly evident analytic and explanatory difficulties. First, how to take conceptual account of the globalization of capital and communications. Second, whether to treat the porousness of state boundaries with regard to drugs, illegal immigration, environmental degradation, unwanted ideas and threats, financial flows and banking operations as posing a fundamentally new series of questions about the nature and effectiveness of sovereignty as the basic approach to the distribution of

authority on a global basis. And third, the extent to which generalized descriptive narratives about the economic/political/legal conditions of the people of the world homogenized crucial differences or illuminated vital affinities (Falk 1993:627).

Thus, Falk asserts, "the main statist/market project of the North is to sustain geopolitical stability, which in turn calls for the continuous expansion of world trade, on economic growth, and on the suppression of nationalist and regionalist challenges emanating from the South, by force if necessary" (1993:628). In this regard, Falk adds, "the internationalization of the state, assuredly a strong tendency, can either be a vehicle for promoting emancipatory or oppressive results" (1993:628). Consequently, "domestic and transnational forces—from society to market activity—will exert various kinds of pressure on the state, often at cross-purposes" (Falk 1993:628).

It is suggested here that various kinds of pressure on developing countries have been felt in the area of language usage. The frequently cited factors for this pressure, as mentioned earlier, include migration, industrialization, school language, urbanization, prestige, and smaller population.

SOCIOLOGICAL FACTORS

In this subsection, instead of discussing each social factor accelerating language deaths in developing countries individually, evidence is provided that highlight these factors together. This is necessary in order to avoid extensive repetitiveness in citing the sources of the evidence.

Until recently, it was feasible for a small speech community to survive in reasonable isolation, to preserve its own language, and to use a language of wider currency for communication with the outside world where necessary. But the growing centralization of life in the 20th century makes this kind of situation increasingly rare. The extent of language death, in particular, is undergoing rapid acceleration in the modern world (Comrie et al. 1996:14).

The speed with which a language can die in developing societies is truly remarkable. Within a generation, all traces of a language can become obsolete. Political decisions can force ethnic groups to move or split up, economic prospects can attract younger members away from the villages, and new diseases can take their toll. As Crystal recounts,

> In 1962, Trumai, spoken in a single village on the lower Culuene River in Venezuela, was reduced by an influenza epidemic to a population of fewer than 10 speakers. In the 19th century, there were thought to be over 1,000 Indian languages in Brazil; today, there are only 200. A quarter of the world's languages have fewer than 1,000 speakers; half have fewer than 10,000. It is likely that most of these languages will die out in the next 50 years (1997:47).

In Tanzania, younger people are increasingly abandoning their mother tongues in favor of Swahili, the dominant language of the country (Comrie 1996:14). Swahili has become so prominent in Tanzania that no other language (including English, an official colonial language of the country) can compete with it in terms of usage.

An assessment of continuity and change in the last stage of the moribund dialect called Negerhollands in the Dutch West Indies sketches the demise of a language in contact. The last speaker's language history and vowel system and an assessment of the variation in a Negerhollands' corpus show how rapid changes in the modern world can accelerate sociological factors that lead to the death of a language (Sabino 1996).

Field data collected from the last remaining speaker of Hukumina and from the last four speakers of Kayeli spoken on the Indonesia island of Buru reveal a series of social factors contributing to the death of the two languages. A significant historical event set in motion changing social dynamics that forced the relocation by the Dutch in 1656 of a number of coastal communities on the island of Buru and other surrounding islands. This severed the ties between Hukumina speakers and their place of origin (with its access to ancestors and associated power). The same event brought a large number of outsiders to reside around the Dutch fort near the traditional village of Kayeli, leading to the creation of a multiethnic and multilingual community that gradually resulted in a shift to Malay for both Hukumina and Kayeli language communities. Supporting evidence from other languages in the area also shows that traditional notions of place and power are tightly linked to language ecology in the region (Grimes 1995).

A sociocultural profile of the Ormuri and Paraci language speakers in southeast Iran shows how accelerated global pressures are impinging upon the two languages. Information concerning their past, present, and future indicates the disappearance on the dialectological level (Kieffer 1977).

Large numbers of Spanish words are used by speakers of Tlaxcalan Nahuatl, an indigenous language of Mexico. As speakers of these languages think it is more advantageous to improve their Spanish, their increasing use of relexification is contributing to the death of the language (Hill 1977).

It is evident from the preceding discussion that language users are interactionally related in a linguistic framework, and their sociological predisposition to language usage is organized and managed in a global domain. All of these structures provide a framework within which any single language choice is produced. Although integrated in a global arena, these structures are conceptually distinct local contexts for each linguistic transaction; that is, local linguistic domains in which a transaction is situated. It is these contexts to which linguistics provides a pathway—and thus, these contexts are the ones which a language analyst can discover through analyzing language usage.

BIBLIOGRAPHY

Afrika, Llaila Olela. 1989. *The Gullah: A People Blessed by God*. Beaufort, SC: Llaila Olela Afrika.

Ammon, Ulrich. ed. 1989. *Status and Function of Languages and Language Varieties*. Berlin and New York: Walter de Gruyter, inc.

Aptheker, H. 1964. *Soul of the Republic: The Negro Today*. New York: Marzani and Munsell.

Asante, Molefi Kete. 1990. African elements in African-American English. In Joseph E. Holloway, ed. *Africanisms in American   Culture*. Bloomington: Indiana University Press.

Austin, J. L. 1962. *How to do Things with Words*. Cambridge, MA.: Harvard University Press.

Awoonor, K. N. 1990. *Ghana: A Political History*. Accra: Sedco Publishing Ltd. and Woeli Publishing Service.

Bangura, Abdul Karim. In progress. Linguistic Connections Between African and African American Languages.

Bangura, A. K. 1994. *Research Methodology and African Studies*. Lanham, MD: University Press of America.

Bangura, Abdul Karim. 1990. Suspension illustrates suppression of African dialect. *The Hilltop* (October 26, p.4).

Bass, L. R. 1979. The Constitution as Symbol: The interpersonal sources of meaning of a secondary symbol. *American Journal of Political Science* vol. 23, no. 1.

Barron, Charles. 1996. Let's get hooked on "Ebonics"! *Educational Cyber Playground*. Accessed: February 21, 2005.

Bastide, Roger. 1971. *African Civilizations in the New World*, trans. Peter Green. London: C. Hurst.

Baugh, John. 2000. *Beyond Ebonics: Linguistic Pride and Racial Prejudice*. Oxford: Oxford University Press.

Blackshire-Belay, Carol Aisha. ed. 1996. *The African-German Experience: Critical Essays*. Westport, CT: Greenwood Publishing Group.

Blight, James G. And Aaron Belkin. 1993. USSR's Third World orphans: Deterring desperate dependents. *Third World Quarterly* 13, 4:715-726.

Bluedom, A. C. 1995. *Organizational Culture*. New York: Hill, Inc.

Branch, Taylor. 1988. *Parting the Waters*. New York: Simon and Schuster.

Brooks, T. 1984. *America's Black Musical Heritage*. Englewood Cliffs, NJ: Prentice-Hall, Inc.

Bull, Tove. 1990. Teaching school beginners to read and write in the vernacular. In *Tromso Linguistics in the Eighties* 11:69-84. Oslo: Novus Press.

Burling, Robbins.1973. *English in Black and White*. Orlando, FL: Holt, Rinehart, and Winston.

Cassidy, F. G. And R. B. LePage. 1980. *Dictionary of Jamaican English*. London: Cambridge University Press.

Columbia University Press. 2003. *The Columbia Electronic Encyclopedia*, 6th ed.

Cobb, R. and C. Elder. 1976. Symbolic identification and political behavior. *American Politics Quarterly* vol. 4:305-332.

Cuny-Hare, M. 1936/1974. *Negro Musicians and Their Music*. New York: Da Capo Press.

Daglish Gerald M. 1972. *A dictionary of Africanisms: Contributions of Sub-Saharan Africa to the English language*. Westport: Greenwood Press.

Dalby, David. 1969. *Black through White: Patterns of Communication in Africa and the New World*. Hans Wolff Memorial Lecture.

DeBose, Charles E. 1991. English grammar from an Afrocentric perspective (paper presented at the conference on The Inclusive University: Multicultural Perspectives in Higher Education, Oakland, California, November 7-10).

Denison, Norman. 1977. Language death or language suicide? *International Journal of the Sociology of Language* 12:13-22.

Dillard, J. L. 1977. *Lexicon of Black English*. New York: Seabury Press.

Dillard, J. L. 1976. *Black Names*. The Hague: Mouton.

Dillard, J. L. 1975. *All-American English*. New York: Random House.

Dorian, Nancy. 1981. *Language Death: The Life Cycle of a Scottish Gaelic Dialect*. Philadelphia: University of Pennsylvania Press.

Dorian, Nancy. 1980. Language shift in community and individual: The phenomenon of the Laggard semi-speaker. *International Journal of the Sociology of Language* 25:85-94.

Dressler, Wolfgang. 1972. On the phonology of language death. *Papers from the Eighth Regional Meeting of the Chicago Linguistic Society*. Chicago: Chicago Linguistic Society.

Dressler, Wolfgang and Ruth Wodak-Leodolter.1977. Language preservation and language death in Brittany. *International Journal of the Sociology of Language* 12:31-44.

Easton, David. 1965. *A framework for Political Analysis*. Englewood Cliffs, New Jersey: Prentice-Hall.

Edelman, M. 1964. *The Symbolic Uses of Politics*. Urbana: The University of Illinois Press.

Elder, C. and R. Cobb. 1983. *The Political Uses of Symbols*. New York: Longman.

Falk, Richard. 1993. Democratising, internationalising, and globalising: A collage of blurred images. *Third World Quarterly* 13, 4:627-640.

Fanon, Frantz. 1967. *Black Skin, White Masks*. New York: Grove Press, Inc.

Fasold, Ralph. 2003. The social construction of 'a language.' Annual lecture of the North West Center for Linguistics, University of Manchester, United Kingdom, April 7.

Fasold, Ralph W. 1999. Ebonic need not be English. *Issue Paper Digest*. Washington, DC: Center for Applied Linguistics.

Fasold, Ralph. 1984. *The Sociolinguistics of Society*. New York: Basil Blackwell, Inc.

Filmore, C. J. 1968. The case for case. E. Bach and R. Harms, eds. *Universals in Linguistic Theory*. New York: Holt Reinhart and Winston.

Filmore, C. J. 1968. An Alternative to Checklist Theories of Meaning (Proceedings of the first annual meeting of the Berkeley Linguistic Society, University of California).

Fishman, Joshua. 1964. Language maintenance and language shift as fields of inquiry. *Linguistics* 9:32-70.

Foner, E. ed. 1976. *America's Black Past*. New York: Harper and Row, Publishers.

Frazier, E. F. 1963. *The Negro Church in America*. Boston: Beacon Press.

Frege, G. 1892/1952. On sense and reference. P. T. Geach and M. Black, eds. *Translations from the Philosophic Writings of Gottlob Frege*. Oxford: Blackwell.

Frazier, E. Franklin. *The Negro Church in America*. Boston: Beacon Press.

Fromkin, Victoria, Robert Rodman and Nina M. Hyams. 2002. *Itroduction to Language*. London: Heinle Group.

Fromkin, V. and R. Rodman. 1998. *An Introduction to Language*, 6th ed. Fort Worth, TX: Harcourt College.

Gal, Susan. 1979. *Language Shift: Social Determinants of Linguistic Change in Bilingual Austria*. New York: Academic Press.

Gazdar, G. 1979. *Pragmatics: Implicature, Presupposition and Logical Form*. New York: Academic Press.

Gold, Robert S. 1960. *A Jazz Lexicon*. New York: Knopf.

Goss, Linda and Marian E. Barnes. 1989. *Talk that Talk: An Anthology of African-American Storytelling*. New York: Simon and Schuster, Inc.

Green, Lisa 2002. *African American English: A Linguistic Introduction*. Cambridge: Cambridge University Press.

Grice, H. P. 1957. Meaning. *Philosophical Review* 64:377-388.

Hanley, Charles J. 1996. A rainbow of languages edging toward oblivion. *Ugabusiness* (August, pp.15-16).

Harry, Beth and Mary G. Anderson. 1994. The disproportionate placement of African American males in special education programs: A critique of the process. *Journal of Negro Education*.

Helfand, Duke. March 24, 2005. Nearly half of Blacks, Latinos drop out, school study shows. *Times*.

Herskovits, Melville J. 1941. *The Myth of the Negro Past*. Boston: Beacon Press.

Holloway, Joseph E. Ed. 1990. *Africanisms in American Culture*. Bloomington: Indiana University Press.

Holloway, Joseph E. And Winifred K. Vass. 1993. *The African   Heritage of American English*. Bloomington: Indiana University   Press.

Holm, John A. and Alison Watt Shilling. 1982. *The Dictionary of Bahamian English*. Cold Spring, NY: Lexik House.

Hoover, Mary Rhodes et al. 1996. African American English tests for students. In Reginald L. Jones, ed. *Handbook of Tests and Measurements for Black Populations*, Vol. 1. Hampton, Virginia: Cobb and Henry Publishers.

Hoover, Mary Rhodes et al. 1996. Tests of African American English for teachers of bidialectal students. In Reginald L. Jones, ed. *Handbook of Tests and Measurements for Black Populations*, Vol. 1. Hampton, Virginia: Cobb and Henry Publishers.

Hoover, Mary Rhodes et al. 1996. African American English attitude measures for teachers. In Reginald L. Jones, ed. *Handbook of Tests and Measurements for Black Populations*, Vol. 1. Hampton, Virginia: Cobb and Henry Publishers.

Huffines, M. Lois. 1980. Pennsylvania German: Maintenance and shift. *International Journal of the Sociology of Language* 25:42-58.

Hull, R. W. 1972. *Munyakare: African Civilization Before the Batuuree*. New York: John Wiley and Sons, Inc.

Irvine, Judith T. and Susan Gal. 2000. Language and ideology and linguistic differentiation. In Paul V. Kroskrity, ed. *Regimes of Language: Ideologies, Politics and Identities*. Sante Fe, NM: School of American Research Press.

Jablin, Frederic et al. 1979. *Handbook on Organizational Communication: An Interdisciplinary Perspective*. London: Sage Publications.

Jamaican Government Public Relations Office. n.d. The Jamaican Directory of Personalities. Kingston, Jamaica: City Printery, Inc.

Johnson, G. B. and R. R. Campbell. 1981. *Black Migration in America*. Durham, NC: Duke University Press.

Johnson, J. W. 1925. *Book of American Negro-Spirituals*. New York: Viking Press.

Jones, E. 1964. The Psychology of Constitutional Monarchy. E. Jones, ed. *Essays in Applied Psycho-Analysis*. London: The Hogart Press.

Jordan, Winthrop D. 1968. *White over Black*. Chapel Hill: University of North Carolina Press.

Ka, Omar. 1995. African language instruction in the United States: Old challenges, new ideas. *African Language Studies in Transition Conference Proceedings*. Princess Anne: University of Maryland Eastern Shore.

Kahane, Henry and Renée Kahane. 1979. Decline and survival of Western prestige languages. *Language* 55, 1:183-198.

Karttunen, L. 1973. Presuppositions of compound sentences. *Linguistic Inquiry* vol. iv, no. 2.

Karttunen, L. 1971. Implicative verbs. *Language* vol. 47.

Keller, Bruce. ed. 1989. *The Harlem Renaissance: A Historical Dictionary from the Era*. Westport: Greenwood Press.

Keto, Tsehloane C. 1991. *The African-centered Perspective: An Introduction*. New Jersey: K. A. Publishers.

Khan, Haider A. 1997. *African Debt and Sustainable Development: Policies for Partnership with Africa*. New York: Phelp-Stokes Fund Africa Papers.

Klingberg, Frank J. 1941. *The Appraisal of the Negro in Colonial South Carolina*. Washington, DC: Associated Publishers.

Kloss, Heinz. 1967. Abstand language and Ausbau languages. *Anthropological Linguistics* 9:29-41.

Kloss, Heinz. 1966. Types of multilingual communities: A discussion of ten variables. *Sociological Inquiry* 36:135-145.

Kochman, T. 1981. *Black and White Styles in Conflict*. Chicago: University of Chicago Press.

Lasswell, H. 1965. *World Politics and Personal Insecurity*. New York: The Free Press.

Levine, Lawrence W. 1977. *Black Culture and Black Consciousness: Afro-American Folk Thought from Slavery to Freedom*. New York: Oxford University Press.

Levinson, S. 1983. *Pragmatics*. Cambridge: Cambridge University Press.

Lewis, E. Glyn. 1978. Migration and the decline of the Welsh language. Joshua Fishman, ed. *Advances in the Study of Societal Multilingualism*. The Hague: Mouton.

Lewis, E. Glyn. 1972. Migration and language in the USSR. Joshua Fishman, ed. *Advances in the Sociology of* Language, vol. 2. The Hague: Mouton.

Lieberson, Stanley and Edward McCabe. 1978. Domains of language usage and mother tongue shift in Nairobi. *International Journal of the Sociology of Language* 18:69-82.

Lyons, J. 1977. *Semantics*. Cambridge: Cambridge University Press.

Major, Clarence. 1978. *Dictionary of Afro-American Slang*. New York.

Malcolm X. 1967. *On Afro-American History*. New York: Pathfinder.

Mazrui, A. A. 1977. *Africa's International Relations*. Boulder, Colorado: Westview Press.

McCrum, Robert, William Cran, and Robert Macneil. 1986. *The Story of English*. New York: Viking Penguin.

Meli, F. 1988. *A History of the ANC: South Africa Belongs to Us*. Harare: Zimbabwe Publishing House.

Merelman, R. 1966. Learning and legitimacy. *American Political Science Review* vol. 60:553-561.

Miller, Randall M. And John David Smith. eds. *Dictionary of Afro-American Slavery*. Westport: Greenwood Press.

Mintz, Sidney W. 1974. *Caribbean Transformations*. Chicago: Aldine.

Mintz, Sidney W. And Richard Price 1976. *An Anthropological Approach to the Afro-American Past: A Caribbean Perspective*. Philadelphia: ISHI.

Moreno Fraginals, Manuel. 1984. *Africa in Latin America: Essay on History*. New York: Holmes and Meier.

Mufwene, S. S., J. R. Rickford, G. Bailey, and J. Baugh, eds. 1998. *African-American English: Structure, History and Use*. London: Routledge.

Orata, Pedro T. 1953. The Iloilo experiment in education through the vernacular. In Unesco, *The Use of Vernacular Languages in Education*. Paris: Unesco Publications.

Osterberg, Tore. 1961. *Bilingualism and the First School Language—An Educational Problem Illustrated by Results from a Swedish Dialect Area*. Umea: Vaster-bottens Tryckeri.

OUSD. 1996. *Synopsis of the Adopted Policy on Standard American English Language Development*. Oakland: Oakland Unified School District (Internet).

Parker, Henry H. and Marilyn I. Crist. 1995. *Teaching Minorities to Play the Corporate Language Game*. Columbia, SC: National Resource Center for the Freshman Year Experience and Students in Transition, University of South Carolina.

Parrinder, G. 1969. *Religion in Africa*. London: Penguin Books.

Poplack, Shana, ed. 2000. *The English History of African American English*. Malden, MA: Blackwell.

Puckett, Newbell Niles. 1975. *Black Names in America: Origins and Usage*. Boston: G. K. Hall.

Pullum, Geoffret K. 1997. Language that dare not speak its name. *Nature*. March 27.

Quarles, B. 1964. *The Negro in the Making of America* (rev ed). New York: Cotier Macmillan Publishers.

Rickford, John R. and Russell J. Rickford. 2000. *Spoken Soul: The Story of Black English*. New York: John Wiley.

Rickford, John R. 1997. Suite for ebony and phonics. *Discover*. December: 82-87.

Rickford, John R. 1997. Using the vernacular to teach the standard. Paper presented at the California State University Long Beach Conference on Ebonics, March 29.

Rickford, John R. 1997. S.B. 205—well-intentioned but uninformed. *Los Angeles Times*. March 28.

Robertson, Tatsha. Saturday, October 4, 2003. Colonial African-Americans' set for reburial. *Boston Globe*.

Russell, B. 1905. On denoting. *Mind* vol. 14:479-493.

Russell, B. 1957. Mr. Strawson on referring. *Mind* vol. 66:385-389.

Senior, O. 1983. *A-Z of Jamaican Heritage*. Kingston, Jamaica: Heinemann Educational Books (Caribbean) Ltd., The Gleaner Company Ltd. (printed and bound by Montrose Printery Ltd., Kingston, Jamaica).

Simpkins, Gary A. and Charlesetta Simpkins. 1981. Cross cultural approach to curriculum development. In Geneva Smitherman, ed. *Black English and the Education of Black Children and Youth: Proceedings of the National Invitational Symposium on the King Decision*, 11-36. Detroit: Center for Black Studies, Wayne State University.

Singham, A. W. and N. L. Singham. 1976. Jamaica. *The World Book Encyclopedia*, vol. 11:J-K. Chicago: Field Enterprises Educational Corporation.

Smith, Jeremy. 1996. *Historical Study of English: A Dynamic Approach*. New York: Routledge.

Smitherman, Geneva. 2000. *Black Talk: Words and Phrases from the Hood to the Amen Corner*. New York: Houghton Mifflin.

Smitherman, Geneva. 1977. *Talking and Testifying: The Language of Black America*. Detroit: Wayne State University Press.

Spencer, J. M. 1990. *Protest and Praise: Sacred Music of Black Religion*. Minneapolis: Portress Press.

Stalnaker, R. C. 1974. Pragmatic presuppositions. M. K. Munitz and P. K. Unger, eds. *Semantics and Philosophy*. New York: New York University Press.

Stalnaker, R. C. 1978. Assertion. P. Cole, ed. *Syntax and Semantics 9: Pragmatics*. New York: Academic Press.

Strawson, P. 1950. On referring. *Mind* vol. 59:320-344.

Strawson, P. 1952. *Introduction to Logical Theory*. London: Metheun.

Stuckey, Sterling. 1987. *Slave Culture: Nationalist Theory and Foundations of Black America*. New York: Oxford University Press.

Tabouret-Keller, Andre. 1972. A contribution to the sociological study of language maintenance and language shift. Joshua Fishman, ed. *Advances in the Sociology of Language*, vol. 2. The Hague: Mouton.

Tabouret-Keller, Andre. 1968. Sociological factors of language maintenance and language shift: A methodological approach based on European and African examples. Joshua Fishman, Charles Ferguson and Jyotirindra Das Gupta, eds. *Language Problems of Developing Nations*. New York: John Wiley and Sons.

Taylor, A. 1976. *Travail and Triumph*. Westport, CT: Greenwood Press.

Taylor, Hanni U. 1989. *Standard English, Black English, and Bidialectalism*. New York: Peter Lang.

Taylor, J. E. 1975. Something on my mind: A cultural and historical interpretation of spiritual texts. *Ethnomusicology* vol. xix, no. 3, September.

Thiong'o, Ngũgĩ wa. 1986. *Decolonising the Mind*. New Hampshire: Heinemann.

Timm, Lenora. 1980. Bilingualism, diglossia and language shift in Brittany. *International Journal of the Sociology of Language* 25:29-42.

Trudgill, Peter. 2001. *Sociolinguistics: An Introduction to Language and Society*, 4th ed. New York: Penguin Group.

Trudgill, Peter and Lars-Gunnar Andersson. 1992. *Bad Language*. New York: Penguin Group.

Trudgill, Peter. 1974. *Sociolinguistics*. New York: Penguin Books.

Tserdanelis, Georgios and Wai Yi Peggy Wong. 2004. *Language Files* 9th ed. Columbus, OH: The Ohio State University Press.

Tshudi, S and L. Thomas. 1998. *The English Language: An Owner's Manual*. Boston: Allyn and Bacon.

Turner, Lorenzo D. 1949/1969. *Africanisms in the Gullah Dialect*. Chicago/New York: University of Chicago Press/Arno Press.

Twiggs, Robert D. 1973. *Pan-African Language in the Western Hemisphere: A Redefinition of Black Dialect as a Language and the Culture of Black Dialect*. North Quincy, MA: Christopher.

Vass, Winifred Kellersberger. 1979. *The Bantu Speaking Heritage of the United States*. Los Angeles: Center for Afro-American Studies, UCLA.

Vaughn-Cook, Fay Boyd. 1987. *American Speech* 62.1.

Wall Street Area Tour. *Radical Walking Tours: Wall Street Area Highlights*. Accessed: March 3, 2005.

Vlahos, O. 1967. *African Beginnings*. Greenwich, Connecticut: Fawcett Publications, Inc.

Walker, D. 1892/1965. Appeal to the coloured citizens of the world. Herbert Aptheker, ed. *One Continual Cry: David Walker's Appeal to the Coloured Citizens of the World (1929-1930), its Setting and its Meaning*. New York: Humanities Press.

Washington Post, The. January 6, 1997. Ebonics: A way to close the learning gap? (pp.A1, A10).

Washington Post, The. January 6, 1997. Among linguists, Black English gets respect (p.A10).

Washington Post, The. December 25, 1996. US bilingual funds ruled out for Ebonics speakers (p.A2).

Weinberg, Meyer. 1977. *Minority Students: A Research Appraisal*. Washington, DC: United States Government Printing Office.

Weinstein, Brian. 1983. *The Civic Tongue*. New York: Longman, Inc.

Whatley, Elizabeth.1981. *Language Among Black Americans*. Language in the USA. Cambridge: Cambridge University Press.

Whitten, Norman E. Jr. and John F. Szwed.1970. *Afro-American Anthropology: Contemporary Perspectives*. New York: Free Press.

Williams, Robert L. ed. 1975. *Ebonics: The True Language of Black Folks*. St. Louis, MO: Institute of Black Studies.

Witvliet, T. 1987. *The Way of the Black Messiah*. Oak Park, IL: Meyer, Stone, and Company, Inc.

Wolfram, Walt and Erik R. Thomas. 2002. *The Development of African American English*. Malden, MA: Blackwell.

Wolfram, W., C. T. Adger and D. Christian. 1999. *Dialects in Schools and Communities*. Mahwah, NJ: Erlbaum.

Wolfram, W. and N. Schilling-Estes. 1998. *American English*. Oxford: Blackwell.

Wood, Peter H. 1974. *Black Majority: Negroes in Colonial South Carolina from 1670 through the Stono Rebellion*. New York: Knopf.

Woodson, Carter G. 1933. *Miseducation of the Negro*. Washington, DC: The Associated Publishers, Inc.

ENDNOTES

1. Presuppositions refer to background assumptions against which the main import of utterances or statements can be assessed (Levinson 1983:173).
2. The term linguistic framework as used here refers to a way of studying various aspects of human language and its interaction with other areas of human culture and behavior, which calls for collecting pertinent data concerning a range of linguistic phenomena, observing the patterns which underlie those phenomena, and expressing the observed regularities by means of certain linguistic rules.
3. According to Elder and Cobb (1983:28), "A symbol is any object used by human beings to index meanings that are not inherent in, nor discernible from, the object itself."
4. Interested readers can find greater details in Gazdar (1979) and Levinson (1983).
5. *Modus ponens* refers to the inference from p~q and ~p to ~q.
6. *Bivalence* refers to the assumption (pv~p) that a presupposition must be either true or false.
7. *Modus tollens* refers to the inference from p~q and q~ to ~p.
8. *Deictic Context* refers to the speech event in which languages encode or grammaticalize linguistic features. The traditional categories of deixis are person, place, and time (Levinson 1983:54,62). To these traditional categories, Lyons (1977) and Filmore (1968, 1975) add discourse (or text) deixis and social deixis.
9. Levinson (1983:181-185) summarizes thirteen presupposition triggers: definite descriptions, factive verbs, implicative verbs, change of state verbs, iteratives, verbs of judging, temporal clauses, cleft sentences, implicit clefts with stressed constituents, comparison and contrasts, non-restrictive relative clauses, counterfactual conditionals, and questions.
10. The earlier view that African religion was crudely fetishistic, with an idea of God where s/he existed being an importation, has long been replaced by the view that most Africans have had the belief in a Supreme Being as an integral part of their worldview and practiced religion long before the arrival of the White man. Missionaries found, often to their surprise, that they did not need to convince Africans about the existence of God, or faith in a life after death, for both these fundamentals of world religion were deeply rooted in Africa before their arrival.
11. The use of the word 'Spirit' here refers to a supernatural being of a certain (good or evil) character. This differs from the earlier use of 'spirit' (as in 'God raises up one's spirits') which refers to vivacity, courage, vigor, enthusiasm, etc.

ABOUT THE AUTHOR

Abdul Karim Bangura is Professor of Research Methodology and Political Science at Howard University and Researcher-In-Residence on Abrahamic Connections and Peace Studies at the Center for Global Peace at American University in Washington, DC. He holds a PhD in Political Science, a PhD in Development Economics, a PhD in Linguistics, and a PhD in Computer Science. He is the author of 61 books and approximately 500 scholarly articles. He is the winner of numerous teaching and other scholarly and community service awards. He is a member of many scholarly organizations and a former President and then United Nations Ambassador of the Association of Third World Studies. He is fluent in a dozen African and six European languages, and is studying to strengthen his proficiency in Arabic, Hebrew, and Hieroglyphics.

CPSIA information can be obtained at www.ICGtesting.com
Printed in the USA
LVOW050434151211

259421LV00022B/3/P